Rhode Island

RHODE ISLAND
BY ROAD

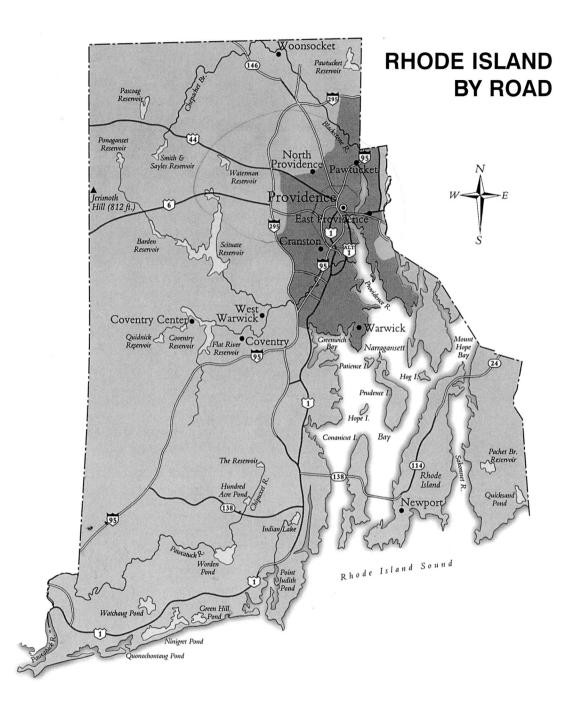

N
W   E
S

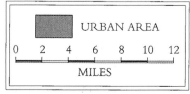

URBAN AREA

0   2   4   6   8   10   12

MILES

Woonsocket

Pawtucket Reservoir

Pascoag Reservoir

Chepachet Br.

Ponaganset Reservoir

Smith & Sayles Reservoir

North Providence

Pawtucket

Blackstone R.

Waterman Reservoir

Jerimoth Hill (812 ft.)

Providence

East Providence

Barden Reservoir

Scituate Reservoir

Cranston

ALT 1

Providence R.

Coventry Center

West Warwick

Warwick

Quidnick Reservoir

Coventry Reservoir

Flat River Reservoir

Coventry

Greenwich Bay

Narragansett

Mount Hope Bay

Patience I.

Hog I.

Prudence I.

Hope I.

The Reservoir

Conanicut I.

Bay

Pachet Br. Reservoir

Hundred Acre Pond

Chipuxet R.

Rhode Island

Saconnet R.

Quicksand Pond

Indian Lake

Newport

Paucatuck R.

Worden Pond

Point Judith Pond

Rhode Island Sound

Watchaug Pond

Green Hill Pond

Pawcatuck R.

Ninigret Pond

Quonochontaug Pond

Block Island

Celebrate the States

Rhode Island

Ted Klein

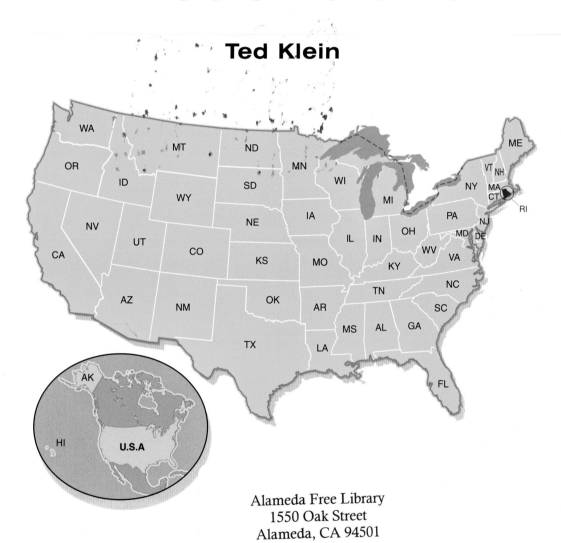

 **Marshall Cavendish**
Benchmark
New York

Marshall Cavendish Benchmark
99 White Plains Road
Tarrytown, NY 10591-9001
www.marshallcavendish.us

All Internet sites were correct and accurate at the time of printing.

Library of Congress Cataloging-in-Publication Data
Klein, Ted.
Rhode Island / by Ted Klein.—2nd ed.
p. cm.—(Celebrate the states)
Summary: "Provides comprehensive information on the geography, history, wildlife,
governmental structure, economy, cultural diversity, peoples, religion, and landmarks of
Rhode Island"—Provided by publisher.
Includes bibliographical references and index.
ISBN 978-0-7614-2560-1
1. Rhode Island—Juvenile literature. I. Title. II. Series.
F79.3.K58 2007
974.5—dc22   2006036490

Editor: Christine Florie
Publisher: Michelle Bisson
Art Director: Anahid Hamparian
Series Designer: Adam Mietlowski

Photo Research by Connie Gardner

Cover photo by agefotostock/SuperStock

The photographs in this book are used by permission and through the courtesy of:
Corbis: Bob Krist, back cover, 19, 103, 135, 136; Catherine Karnow, 12, 100; Tom Stewart, 21;
D. Robert Franz, 22; Bettmann, 45, 127, 128; Rose Hartman, 49; Wally McNamee, 52; David
H. Wells, 61, 91; Reuters, 76, 126; Bob Rowan, 80, 83, 88, 119; Ray Stubblebine, 85; Rick Friedman,
87; Lee Snider, 97; Leo Mason, 104; Kelley Mooney Photography, 106; Onne Van der Val, 108;
Joe McDonald, 114; Pam Gardner, 115; Nik Wheeler, 121; Barney Burstein, 130; *PhotoEdit:*
Susan Van Etten, 111; *Getty Images:* Steve Dunwell/Image Bank, 8; Christian Science Monitor, 59; Ira
Block/National Geographic, 102; George Benson, 123; *The Image Works:* David H. Wells, 57;
Andre Jenny, 66; Pat Watson, 81; *Kindra Clineff:* 50, 55, 92; *SuperStock:* James Lemass, 10,
Raymond Forbes, 94; David Forbert, 99, 103; *Dembinsky Photo Associates:* Fritz Polking, 13; *The
Image Works:* David H. Wells, 16; *AP Photo:* Steve Milne, 24, 68; Victoria Arocho, 62, 73; A.
Giblin, 64; AP Photo, 69; *The Granger Collection:* 26, 30, 41, 46; *NorthWind Picture Archive:* 28,
33, 34, 37, 38, 39; *Alamy:* Maggie Janik, 17; Joe Sohm, 78; Andre Jenny, 96.

Printed in Malaysia
1 3 5 6 4 2

Contents

Rhode Island Is . . .

Rhode Island is a land that was given in friendship by the Native Americans, not bought or stolen.

"The truth is, not a penny was demanded. . . . It was not price nor money that could have purchased Rhode Island. Rhode Island was obtained by love."
—Roger Williams, founder of Providence, 1636

Rhode Island is proud of its past . . .

"Every house in this town seems to have a historical plaque on it, and every street seems to have its own story."
—Newport native Marlene Finn Gabriel

. . . but some parts of its past are disappearing.

"There's not much farmland left here, and no place that feels truly rural. We've just gotten too crowded."
—West Warwick printer Marc Michaud

Rhode Island is home to fiercely independent people.

"Many of us chose Rhode Island over approximately forty-nine other states because it seemed such fertile ground for eccentrics. . . . I looked around at the delightfully odd people I met here and said to myself, this is the place for me."
—writer Nathaniel Reade

Living in the smallest state makes some Rhode Islanders feel inferior . . .

"When you're from the smallest state in a very big country, it's easy to get caught up in believing you're too little to count."
—editorial in *Rhode Island Monthly*

. . . but others appreciate their unusual position.

"Knowing you live in the smallest state in the Union, you tend not to have an inflated sense of your own importance. It keeps you from putting on airs. I think that's one of the things that makes Rhode Islanders so special: we have a sense of humor about ourselves."
—Deborah Newton, knitwear designer

Through hard times and times of plenty, the people of the Ocean State remain endlessly inventive.

"Our state motto 'Hope' . . . is our fundamental frame of mind as we address the future."
—former governor J. Joseph Garrahy

Rhode Island, whose symbol "the Independent Man" sits atop the state's capitol dome, is by far the smallest state in the Union, but it is uniquely rich in history. It was in many ways the most honorable of the original thirteen colonies, but at times the most disreputable. It was the scene of America's first antislavery law, yet the slave trade was a source of its wealth. It was the birthplace of true religious freedom in America, the birthplace of our industrial revolution, the first state to declare independence (a full two months before the rest), and the last original state to ratify the Constitution—because it insisted on a Bill of Rights. Known today for its small-town informality and quirky good humor, Rhode Island still retains its independent spirit.

Chapter One

A Little Universe

The state of Rhode Island—officially nicknamed the Ocean State but affectionately known as Little Rhody—is smaller than many counties, smaller than some national parks, smaller even than Texas's King Ranch. Just 48 miles long and 37 miles wide, it ranks fiftieth in size—only half as big as Delaware, the next-largest state, and less than one five-hundredth the size of Alaska. It's an easy place to explore. Fortunately, there's a lot worth exploring.

CARVED BY GLACIERS

Take a look at a map. Rhode Island's shape resembles an upright rectangle pierced from below by the thin wedge of Narragansett Bay, splintering off the eastern portion of the state. Providence, Rhode Island's biggest city, sits at the top of the bay.

The narrow portion of the state on the eastern side of the bay seems like it should be part of Massachusetts rather than Rhode Island. The town of Tiverton, for example, is connected by land to Massachusetts—and it can't be reached from the main part of Rhode Island without taking a bridge.

Though Rhode Island is small in size, its location on the Atlantic coast provides an abundance of natural beauty.

The bay itself, penetrating 28 miles into the state, is filled with three large islands and dozens of smaller ones, some no more than rocky outcroppings. The largest island, Aquidneck, contains the city of Newport. Another body of land, Block Island, lies 12 miles out at sea.

The coast's ragged look, like the rest of New England's geography, is largely the result of glaciers. About 100,000 years ago, the earth's climate cooled slightly and the polar ice cap began to spread south. As the ice advanced, it picked up rocks and stones. Using these the way a carpenter

Rhode Island's coastline can be rough and ragged in spots.

uses sandpaper, the ice carved out channels that became rivers and bays, and scoured out depressions that later became plains and lakes. Massive chunks of ice were left melting after the glaciers had retreated northward, forming freshwater ponds. Where the rock was strongest and most resistant, such as in the western part of the state, hills were left; where the rock was softest, as in the area east of Narragansett Bay, the land was flattened.

Even at their highest, the hills of Rhode Island are nothing to brag about. The state's highest point, Jerimoth Hill in Foster, near the Connecticut border, rises just 812 feet above sea level. You won't find much downhill skiing or mountain climbing in the Ocean State.

A LAND OF FORESTS

A 1930 travel guide boasted, "The amazing thing about this state is the diversity of its scenery, combining within its borders the lure of the sea and the beauty of the rolling hills." That's still true today. For so small a state, Rhode Island possesses an impressively varied landscape, from the hills in the north and west, to the flat coastal plains east of Narragansett Bay, to the marshes, beaches, and tidal ponds along the southern shore.

In 1524, when the explorer Giovanni da Verrazano first ventured through Rhode Island, he described the woods as "so great and thicke" that an army could have hidden in them. In fact, the state is more wooded today than it was in the nineteenth century, when much of the land was cleared and devoted to farming. More than half of Rhode Island is once again covered with forests of oak, maple, pine, hickory, and other trees. Today, the forests look as if they've been wild forever, but ancient stone walls that mark the boundaries of what were open fields in the eighteenth and nineteenth centuries can still be found.

Rhode Island Forest Conservators Organization is dedicated to the protection of the state's more than 380,000 acres of forest land.

"We have a good mixture of hardwood and softwood," says Brian Tefft, a state wildlife biologist, "but compared with ten years ago it's an *older* forest, with larger trees. I wish we had more diversity." Although the total amount of woodland has been "holding steady" over the past decade, Tefft says, "the biggest threat is development—the conversion of forest land to shopping malls and new homes. Then it's lost forever."

Rhode Island's forests no longer teem with large wildlife, but occasionally a black bear or a moose wanders in from neighboring Massachusetts or Connecticut. There is a growing population of white-tailed deer, as well as smaller animals such as squirrels and chipmunks. An increasing number of coyotes is feeding off the small game and deer.

When natural food sources dwindle, coyote sightings become more frequent.

Ruffed grouse, known in New England as partridges, are plentiful, as are migrating birds such as woodcocks and mourning doves. Wild turkeys, which once thrived in the forests, disappeared in the 1800s because of habitat destruction. "But they were reintroduced to Rhode Island from Vermont in 1980, and now there are around three thousand birds," Tefft says proudly.

What makes the abundance of forests so surprising is that, with more than 960 people per square mile, Rhode Island is the second-most densely populated state, following only New Jersey. Crowding about one million people into 1,045 square miles of land means that the inhabited portions of the state—the parts not occupied by forests or farmland—have undergone a fundamental change in character. Architectural historian William H. Jordy mourned this change, saying that modern-day Rhode Island has lost "the sense of individual villages and town centers, as the towns have spread into a continuous suburb."

Keeping a sense of nature alive even in Rhode Island's largest city was the goal of the Providence Tree Tally, a four-month survey that began in May 2006. Around 30,000 trees grow on the city streets, and the object of the tally was to take an inventory of them all (not including trees on private property). More than one hundred volunteers, including many students, were equipped with tree-identification guides and special tape measures that, when wrapped around the trunk of a tree, indicate the tree's diameter as well as its circumference. For each tree they encountered, volunteers noted its species, size, health, and location, as well as possible obstructions such as power lines. "It turned out to be as much fun as bird-watching," reported one homeowner in the neighborhood around Brown University. "I never paid much attention to the trees around me before, but now I'm much more observant."

LAND AND WATER

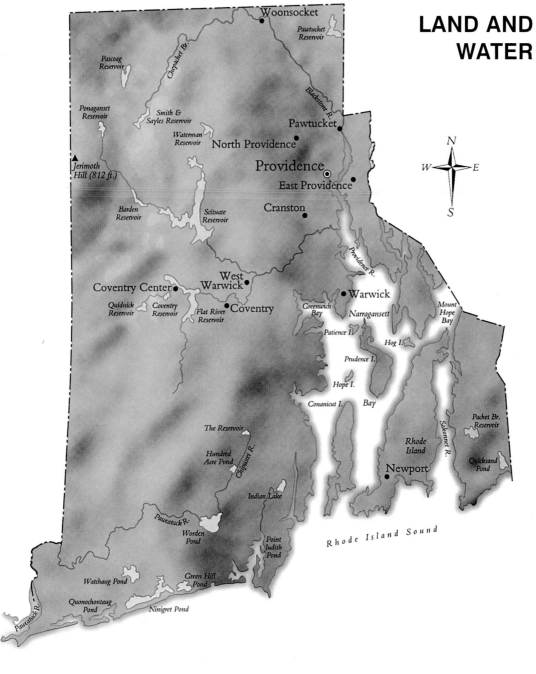

Woonsocket

Pawtucket Reservoir

Pascoag Reservoir

Chepachet Br.

Ponaganset Reservoir

Smith & Sayles Reservoir

Blackstone R.

Waterman Reservoir

Pawtucket

North Providence

Providence

East Providence

▲ Jerimoth Hill (812 ft.)

Barden Reservoir

Scituate Reservoir

Cranston

Providence R.

West Warwick

Coventry Center

Warwick

Quidnick Reservoir

Coventry Reservoir

Flat River Reservoir

Coventry

Greenwich Bay

Narragansett

Patience I.

Hog I.

Mount Hope Bay

Prudence I.

The Reservoir

Hope I.

Conanicut I.

Bay

Hundred Acre Pond

Chipuxet R.

Rhode Island

Sakonnet R.

Pachet Br. Reservoir

Quicksand Pond

Indian Lake

Newport

Pawcatuck R.

Worden Pond

Point Judith Pond

Rhode Island Sound

Watchaug Pond

Green Hill Pond

Quonochontaug Pond

Pawcatuck R.

Ninigret Pond

N
W   E
S

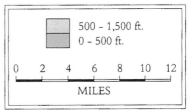

500 – 1,500 ft.

0 – 500 ft.

0   2   4   6   8   10   12

MILES

Block Island

POWERFUL WATERS

Because of the state's tiny size, every town and village in Rhode Island lies within 25 miles of the sea. "Rhode Island is truly an ocean state," wrote newspaperman Stuart Hale. "No resident is more than thirty minutes away by car from the water's edge." It's not surprising that in addition to a state bird, a state flower, and other official symbols, Rhode Island has a state shellfish—a local breed of clam called a quahog.

With more than 400 miles of coastline despite the state's small size, Rhode Island has every variety of shore landscape, from the high, shifting dunes of Watch Hill and the rocky beaches of Little Compton to the broad, flat shores of Newport and Narragansett, which attract huge crowds in the summer.

A local favorite, which also happens to be Rhode Island's state shellfish, is the quahog.

Rhode Island's Narragansett coastline is mostly flat.

Water has been the key to the state's prosperity—the saltwater of the Atlantic Ocean and Narragansett Bay and the freshwater of the rivers and streams that empty into them. The ocean supported the early Rhode Island industries of fishing, boatbuilding, and international trade. The rivers provided power to run the state's first mills. Rhode Island's rivers were particularly valuable because, as one historian noted, they were "fast-moving, almost never frozen, and never dry," and therefore "perfectly adapted for mill wheels to generate steady and certain sources of power." Today, factories no longer depend on water power; like the ocean and the bay, Rhode Island's rivers are used mainly for recreation.

SAVING THE SALT PONDS

The southern edge of Rhode Island is home to an unusual ecosystem: a series of saltwater tidal ponds, which New Englanders call "salt ponds." Some of these ponds are connected to the ocean but are partially sealed off behind long, narrow sandbars; others are closed to the ocean.

Although the ponds cover some 3,700 acres, they average less than 4 feet in depth. This shallowness allows sunlight to penetrate all the way to the bottom of the ponds, promoting the growth of eelgrass and other plants and forming the perfect environment for many species of fish and shellfish, including flounder, quahogs, bay scallops, and oysters. Migratory birds often stop at these ponds for shelter and food.

Rhode Island's salt ponds are endangered. An oil spill in 1996 was the worst in Rhode Island history. A barge ran aground at the Ninigret National Wildlife Refuge and leaked more than 828,000 gallons of home heating oil, polluting five of the ponds. But pollution from homeowners' septic systems is an even greater threat.

Organizations in Rhode Island have begun efforts to maintain the health of the state's salt ponds, which are home to fragile ecosystems.

Because of these dangers, activist Virginia Lee founded the Rhode Island Salt Pond Watchers, a group that monitors the ponds' health by taking water samples. "We are the Ocean State," Lee said, "and environmental quality is a big part of the quality of life for Rhode Islanders."

Thanks to information that Lee's group provided on dangerous levels of bacteria in the water, one of the ponds and portions of two others have been closed to shellfish digging, and new septic regulations have been enacted. Lee's efforts have inspired similar groups as far away as Texas. "There are over a thousand programs now around the country," she said, in which ordinary citizens—many of them schoolchildren—watch over the quality of the air and water around them.

The 1996 oil spill damaged more than just the salt ponds. It killed nine million lobsters and shut down the state's lobster catch for five months, putting many people in the fishing port of Galilee out of work. As part of a $10 million legal settlement between the state and the shipping company responsible for the oil spill, the seabeds in the area were eventually restocked with more than one million female lobsters, and by 1999 the population seemed to have more than come back. However, the following year, the catch began to decline, and it continues to dwindle. Today, the lobster catch is less than one-third of what it was in 1999. Rhode Island lobstermen, like those in neighboring Massachusetts, are now working longer days but pulling up fewer lobsters—and many of those that are caught turn out to be unhealthy, suffering from a disease that pits, blackens, and weakens their shells. The lobsters may be less resistant to disease because of water pollution and perhaps even global warming, but their population has also declined because of a rise in the number of striped bass (the official Rhode Island state fish), which eat baby lobsters. Still another cause of the problem is overfishing, with lobsters being captured at an increasingly young age. As one lobsterman explained to the *Providence Journal*, "It's as if you went into a town each year and took away everyone over the age of thirteen. What are the chances the population that remains is going to thrive?"

Not only shellfish were affected by the oil spill; more than two thousand Rhode Island shore birds were killed as well, including many piping plovers, an endangered species. This shy, extremely rare little bird lays its eggs in the sand. When the eggs hatch, the chicks, unlike those of most species, do not wait for their parents to feed them. Instead, within hours, they follow their parents to the water's edge to feed on insects and tiny crustaceans.

Disasters that threaten the environment off the shores of Rhode Island have jeopardized sea life, particularly lobsters.

"Plovers are quite beautiful, and they're very quick," says a longtime resident of Little Compton who lives near Goosewing Beach, a nesting area. "They run around on their little legs, and when they get startled, they all take off en masse."

A piping plover stands guard over her nest and eggs.

Whether they are scurrying over the beach as babies or nesting in the sand as adults, these birds are naturally vulnerable to predators—other birds, wild animals, and even dogs and cats. They may also be crushed by automobiles driving over the beach. Sunbathers frighten them, and so do kite flyers. To plovers, kites look like birds of prey. Rhode Island has protected this species in five nature preserves, banning—and sometimes roping off or even fencing out—humans, their cars, and their pets from the dunes where plovers are nesting. For these small birds, the key to survival is simple: do not disturb.

A CLIMATE BOTH MILD AND STORMY

Over the years, writers have described Rhode Island's climate as everything from "invigorating and changeable" to "even and excellent throughout the year." In truth, Rhode Island has a wide variety of climates for such a small state. The dry winds of the state's interior create a more severe climate than the gentle sea breezes of the coastal regions. Block Island, for example, enjoys an average annual growing season of 214 days, compared with only 144 days for the landlocked town of Kingston. A blizzard in 1978 left 21 inches of snow on Block Island—but 56 inches in the northern counties on the mainland. Generally, however, the state's snowfall is light for New England. Unlike their neighbors, Rhode Islanders have only a 25 percent chance of a white Christmas each year. "For New England," said native Rhode Islander John Hale, who now lives in Maine, "Rhode Island's about as tropical as you can get."

In the summer, sea breezes keep Rhode Island's coastal areas cooler than places located farther inland. But even inland, the temperature rises above 90 degrees Fahrenheit only about eight days each year.

Typically, Rhode Island enjoys temperate weather, but it is known to experience snow storms during the winter months.

Generally, Rhode Island's climate is so peaceful that, according to National Weather Service statistics, from 1995 to 2005 the state actually enjoyed the lowest number of weather-related fatalities in the nation. (The next safest states were Rhode Island's two neighbors, Connecticut and Massachusetts.) But as a coastal state, Rhode Island does suffer from the weather in one respect: since 1635, it has been devastated by two dozen major hurricanes and hundreds of smaller storms called "nor'easters." A fierce hurricane hit in 1938, causing widespread flooding, 40-foot waves, and winds of 120 miles per hour. It was the worst natural disaster in New England history, leaving more than 600 people dead—317 of them were Rhode Islanders. The state suffered more than $100 million in property damage, and some communities were wiped off the map. *Natural History* magazine noted that one cottage colony on the south shore was "so completely obliterated that pictures taken the morning after show nothing but a long stretch of barren sand." In downtown Providence, the waters rose to 7 feet above street level. Today, a stone barrier wall with three massive 40-foot-wide hurricane gates help protect the city, but a number of buildings throughout the state still bear plaques on their outer walls marking the height of the 1938 flood. "Rhode Islanders are proud of their past," says a European engineer now living in Providence, "even their disasters."

Chapter Two

A Tradition of Independence

Although it is small, Rhode Island is rich in history. The area it now covers was inhabited for thousands of years before the coming of European settlers. Scientists believe that tribes whose ancestors originated in Asia migrated there more than eight thousand years ago.

NATIVE-AMERICAN HERITAGE

By the 1600s, when the European settlers arrived, perhaps 30,000 Native Americans lived there in five main tribes: the Niantic, Nipmuck, Pequot, Wampanoag, and Narragansett. These last two groups were the largest, and they were frequently at war with one another.

Rhode Island's Native Americans moved often, setting up villages near the shore in the summer, where they planted crops and gathered shellfish,

Rhode Island's history begins with the Native-American tribes of the region and clergyman Roger Williams.

and moving to the nearby forest in the winter, where they carved shells into intricately designed beads called "wampum," which they used for money and exchanged with neighboring tribes. Their homes, designed to be easily taken down and moved, were built of bark, animal skin, or straw mats over a framework of poles that were tied together at the top, with a smokehole in the roof. Women had the job of erecting and taking down homes and transporting them when the tribe moved.

Women also did the planting and plowing. Corn was the main crop, along with squash and beans. It was often the children's job to camp out in the cornfields and scare away the early-morning birds. Birds were also kept away by hawks, which the Native Americans captured and trained to prey on the birds that fed on the corn.

Native Americans in Rhode Island received food from the sea, as well as from crops such as corn.

The only crop that the men grew was tobacco. Each man carried a bag of tobacco around his neck and smoked it with a pipe. Throughout the year, the men hunted and fished. Game was abundant, as were wild berries and edible roots. The Native Americans ate well and were healthy, tall, and strong. One study estimates that their diet was far more nutritious than that of the Europeans. As historian Charles C. Mann wrote, early European settlers found the Native Americans "strikingly healthy specimens." They made tools and weapons of chipped stone. They built birch-bark canoes and dugouts—canoes made of hollowed-out logs.

The Native Americans also enjoyed sports, including footraces and contests of skill with tomahawks, spears, and bows and arrows, as well as a game played with a deerskin ball stuffed with moss or leaves that may have been similar to football or soccer. Teams of young men from one village played against teams from other villages on beaches or in meadows, while hundreds of spectators cheered them on and even made bets on the outcome. One historian said, "The first of all football games in this land might well have been played on the shores of Narragansett Bay."

EARLY EXPLORATION

No one can be sure exactly when the first Europeans reached the shores of what is now New England. Viking seafarers from Norway may have explored the region as early as 1000 C.E. The first Europeans known to have set foot in this region came with Giovanni da Verrazano, an Italian sailing on behalf of France, who explored Narragansett Bay in 1524 while searching for a route to Asia.

Verrazano may have indirectly given Rhode Island its name. He is said to have compared one of the local islands—either Aquidneck or, more likely, Block Island—to the Greek island of Rhodes. Other historians say

Giovanni da Verrazano, an Italian navigator, was the first European to explore Narragansett Bay.

that the state's name comes from the Dutch trader Adriaen Block, who sailed to the region in 1614 and called one of the islands *roodt eylandt*, or "red island," because of its red clay shores. Whether Block named the state or not, he did give his name to one place he visited: Block Island.

FOUNDING A COLONY

Americans sometimes assume that the early colonists left England in search of religious freedom, but the word *freedom* can be misleading. The group known as the Pilgrims—who settled in Plymouth, Massachusetts, in 1620—and the Puritans—who settled in the Massachusetts Bay Colony ten years later—sought religious freedom for themselves, not for others. Convinced that their way of worshipping God was the only right way, they were intolerant of anyone who disagreed.

One idealistic young Puritan minister had different ideas. Roger Williams arrived in Boston from England in 1631 and taught at a church in nearby Salem, Massachusetts. Unlike his fellow Puritans, he believed in the idea of separation of church and state. He felt government had no business interfering with religion or enforcing religious laws; that made for bad government and bad religion. He argued that it was wrong for the state to force people to attend church and to honor the Sabbath. "Forced worship stinks in God's nostrils," he said. Religion was a private matter, for each individual to practice as he or she pleased. Williams's independent views, and the courage with which he expressed them, continually got him into trouble.

So did his attitude toward the Native Americans. From the start, he befriended them, traded with them, studied their language and customs, and respected them as human beings. "Nature," he wrote, "knows no difference between European and American [Indian] in blood, birth, bodies, etc."

What especially angered the Puritan authorities was Williams's declaration that the colonists had no right to take the Native Americans' land.

A natural peacemaker who, throughout his life, was called upon again and again to mediate between whites and Native Americans, sometimes at the risk of his own safety, Williams became close friends with Massasoit, the leader of the Wampanoag who lived on the eastern side of Narragansett Bay, and with Canonicus, a leader of the Narragansett who lived on the western side. These men saw Williams almost as a son, even though their tribes were enemies.

In late 1635, Williams learned that the Massachusetts Bay authorities planned to banish him and ship him back to England. With only his faithful servant, Thomas Angell, as a companion, Williams set forth into the snowy wilderness to find a new home. After fourteen weeks of wandering, they settled at Massasoit's winter camp in what would become Rehoboth, Massachusetts. In the spring, they were joined by Williams's wife and children and a few followers. Forbidden to settle in the area—it belonged to the Plymouth Colony, which feared offending its Massachusetts Bay neighbors—Williams and his party paddled across the Seekonk River, searching for a place to live. As legend has it, they spied a group of Native Americans on the western shore who hailed Williams with the amiable greeting, "What cheer, Netop?" ("What news, friend?"). They were Narragansett, and they gladly gave Williams land along the river to found a settlement. In thanks for "God's merciful providence," Williams named the place Providence.

A HAVEN FOR MISFITS

The Providence colony—officially known as Providence Plantations—was meant to be, in Williams's words, "a shelter for persons distressed for conscience," a refuge for those who had been persecuted for their beliefs or who sought religious freedom.

Roger Williams is greeted by the Narragansett upon landing in what was to become Providence.

Inspired by Williams, religious nonconformists—those who disagreed with established religious teaching—began to move into other areas along Narragansett Bay. In 1638 another independent-minded Puritan, Anne Hutchinson—who had been banished by the Massachusetts Bay Colony for preaching fiercely against the established church—settled at Pocasseit, today's Portsmouth, at the northern end of Aquidneck Island. A year later William Coddington broke away from Hutchinson's group and founded a settlement called Newport at the island's southern tip. Samuel Gorton, another ardent believer in religious liberty, founded a village called Sha-womet south of Providence in 1642. Its name was later changed to Warwick.

By this time these towns were thought of as a single colony, "Rhode Island and Providence Plantations." That remains the state's official name today.

In 1643 Roger Williams sailed back to England to obtain an official charter for his colony. During the trip he assembled the notes he had been making for the past twelve years on Native-American speech and customs into a book entitled *A Key into the Language of America*. It became the first published book in English about Native-American life, and it was so useful as a dictionary that three centuries later, an explorer in the wilds of eastern Canada found that it helped him communicate with a tribe he encountered whose language was similar to that of the Narragansett. In the book Williams teaches us, among other things, the words for one to ten (*nquít, neèsse, nìsh, yòh, napànna, qútta, énada, showsuck, paskúgit, piùck*), the word for "child" (*papoòs*), and how to say "I love you" (*Cowàmmaunsh*).

Anne Hutchinson at her sentencing of banishment from the Massachusetts Bay colony in 1637.

Soon the new colony, with its reputation for religious tolerance, was attracting groups such as Quakers and Jews who did not feel welcome in the other colonies. In fact, Rhode Island suffered abuse from its less-tolerant neighbors. To one minister, the place was "the receptacle of all sorts of riff-raff people, and is nothing else than the sewer of New England." Called an "asylum to evil-doers," it was nicknamed "Rogues' Island."

MURDER IN THE TAVERN: A FOLKTALE

Once called "Rogues' Island" by its neighbors, Rhode Island has long had a reputation as a place that harbored misfits and criminals. One such man, Jim Andrews, ran a tavern in the early 1800s, where, as the tale goes, he made lots of money—literally. He was a counterfeiter who employed peddlers traveling throughout the state to pass his phony bills. In the early 1800s counterfeiting money was a crime that was punishable by death.

One night, one of his men burst into the tavern. "The law's after me!" he said. Fearing the man would reveal their scam to the authorities Andrews poured him drink after drink until the man dropped off to sleep. Andrews then silenced him forever by hammering a huge spike through his neck. He buried the body in a nearby swamp. Later, when two boys almost stumbled over the grave, Andrews dug up the body and reburied it behind the tavern. It is said that afterward, on dark nights, people passing the tavern would be stopped by a ghostly stranger who would beg them to help pull the spike from his neck.

Years later, after the tavern was long gone, a boy and his mother were passing the same spot on a moonlit winter's night when newly fallen snow covered the ground. Suddenly they made out a shadowy figure walking ahead of them, tugging at something in his neck. They lost sight of the figure, and when they looked down to see where he had been walking, they could find no footprints in the snow.

WAR WITH THE NATIVE AMERICANS

Roger Williams wanted to be "peaceable" neighbors with the Native Americans. But other colonists, hungry for land, were neither honorable nor neighborly.

By 1674 Massasoit's son Metacomet, known to the colonists as King Philip, had had enough. More than one-third of coastal New England's Native Americans—some historians say as many as 90 percent—had been wiped out by disease since the Europeans had arrived, and King Philip's people, the Wampanoag, had suffered even more than most other tribes. Now they were being pushed off their land by English settlers. "Tract after tract is gone," King Philip said. "But a small part of the dominions of my ancestors remains. I am determined not to live till I have no country."

The Wampanoag began to attack homesteaders. In 1675 the Massachusetts and Connecticut colonies declared war against the Native Americans. Rhode Islanders and the Narragansett tried to stay out of the conflict, which became known as King Philip's War, but they were drawn in when soldiers from the other colonies made a surprise raid on the Narragansett, who they feared might be harboring King Philip. In what was called the Great Swamp Fight, Massachusetts, Connecticut, and Plymouth Colony troops attacked the Narragansett and Wampanoag refugees in the Great Swamp west of what is now Kingston, Rhode Island, in December 1675. The camp was surrounded and burned, and hundreds of Narragansett were killed, including women, children, and the elderly. Their leader, Canonchet, escaped.

Joining the Wampanoag, the Narragansett retaliated by ambushing more than fifty-five white soldiers and their Native-American allies near present-day Central Falls, Rhode Island. They then burned Providence and other towns in the area. Many colonists fled to Aquidneck.

In December 1675 colonists and Native Americans battled in Rhode Island during King Philip's War.

Eventually, in 1676, both Canonchet and King Philip were captured and shot. Although there were occasional skirmishes later, the Native Americans had been conquered. This was the last great Native-American uprising in New England.

SLAVERS AND SMUGGLERS

After King Philip's War some Indians were shipped to southern colonies or to the West Indies as slaves. Rhode Islanders tended to be less tolerant of slavery in their own colony. In 1652 the colony of Rhode Island outlawed any human servitude, whether "blacke mankinde or white," lasting more than ten years. This was America's first antislavery law. However, it did not remain in effect for long.

In time, Newport and Bristol became two of the leading slaveholding cities in New England. Slavery in New England was different from slavery in the South. Households that owned slaves typically had only a few, who performed the same tasks as white servants. They did not simply work in the fields, as was often the case on Southern plantations. They lived closely with the slaveholding family and adopted the family's customs. Because Puritans thought it was important for everyone to understand the Bible, slaves were usually taught to read.

Slaves in the North traditionally performed duties of white servants.

From the start, New Englanders had mixed feelings about slavery. Moses Brown, whose wealthy family was among Providence's most active slave traders, had a change of heart after more than half the slaves died—some from disease, some in an attempted revolt—on a ship that he and his brothers owned. Defying his surly, brawling brother John, the smaller, gentler Moses freed his slaves in 1773 and helped found the Providence Society for Promoting the Abolition of Slavery, for the Relief of Persons Unlawfully Held in Bondage, and for Improving the Conditions of the African Race. "I am clearly convinced," he wrote, "that the buying and selling of men . . . is contrary to the Divine mind."

In 1784 Rhode Island passed a "gradual emancipation act," which stated that present slaves would remain in bondage, but their children would be free. By 1800, less than 1 percent of Rhode Island's population was made up of slaves, and by 1840 there were only five slaves left in the state, elderly men and women living out their last years with the families of their owners.

Until the American Revolution, however, merchants and shipowners in Newport and Providence were heavily involved in the so-called triangular trade: rum from the American colonies was traded in Africa for slaves, the slaves were traded in the West Indies for molasses or sugar, and the molasses or sugar was shipped to Rhode Island and other New England colonies to be made into rum. By 1750 rum was Rhode Island's major manufactured item. Fishing, especially whaling, was its other important industry.

In the 1760s England passed a series of taxes that restricted trade between the colonies and non-British islands in the West Indies. Deprived of molasses from islands owned by France, Spain, and Holland, Rhode Islanders took increasingly to smuggling. In 1764 Rhode Island troops fired on a British ship that was hunting for smugglers as it attempted to leave Newport Harbor. Some historians believe these were the first shots of the American Revolution.

A more famous incident eight years later has also been called the first act of the revolution. On June 9, 1772, a British ship, the *Gaspee*, ran aground in Narragansett Bay while pursuing a Rhode Island boat that was suspected of smuggling. Rhode Islanders, who knew where the shoals were, had lured the larger vessel into waters that were too shallow for it. Late that night, eight boats manned by citizens of Providence attacked the ship. After shooting the *Gaspee*'s captain, the Rhode Islanders boarded the ship, forced the crew into boats, and set the ship ablaze.

Angry Rhode Islanders set the British Gaspee *aflame after it ran aground in Narragansett Bay while chasing a Rhode Island boat suspected of smuggling.*

The wounded captain was rowed to a house onshore. "Bloodstains on the floor," wrote historian William G. McLoughlin, "were pointed out for a century thereafter as 'the first blood of the Revolution.'"

FIRST TO REBEL

Because Rhode Islanders were so heavily involved in trade, British trade restrictions and taxes affected them severely. This made them eager to be free of Great Britain's rule—so eager, in fact, that the colony's General Assembly voted to end its allegiance to England on May 4, 1776, two full months before the other twelve colonies declared their independence.

Despite its eagerness to fight, the colony of Rhode Island saw only one major battle during the revolution, the Battle of Rhode Island. In August 1778 American troops under General John Sullivan attacked the British forces occupying Newport. They fought the British back to the final defenses around Newport, but they were not able to capture the city. The Americans withdrew, pursued by the British. At Portsmouth they successfully fended off a British attack and were able to retreat to safety. A battalion of freed slaves, known as the Black Regiment, fought courageously for the colonists and helped keep the British at bay. It was the first African-American regiment to see combat in America.

THE INDUSTRIAL REVOLUTION

After the American Revolution, Rhode Island maintained its independent spirit. It refused to ratify the U.S. Constitution until ten amendments—the Bill of Rights—were added. At a special convention in May 1790, it finally voted to join the Union. It was the last of the original thirteen colonies to do so. The motion passed by only two votes.

DORR'S REBELLION—A SECOND AMERICAN REVOLUTION

Although Roger Williams was a staunch believer in democracy, Rhode Island lagged behind the other colonies in granting its citizens the right to vote. For much of its history, only adult white male property owners and their eldest sons could vote, which left out more than half the adult white males, to say nothing of nonwhites and women.

Thomas Wilson Dorr (below), a wealthy lawyer, considered this a great injustice to working people. In 1841 he formed a political party, the People's Party, which was dedicated to winning the vote for all men. The party held its own election, allowing all white males to vote. (Dorr wanted African Americans to be included, but he was overruled.) The party adopted a new state constitution and elected Dorr governor of Rhode Island. He was inaugurated in May 1842 in Providence—one day before the legal governor, Samuel Ward King, was inaugurated in Newport. Tiny Rhode Island now had two governors!

The official government refused to recognize Dorr as governor. The People's Party tried to seize the Providence arsenal, where weapons were stored, but troops chased them away. Dorr then attempted to raise a revolutionary army. When he failed to attract enough support, he gave himself up and eventually spent a year in prison.

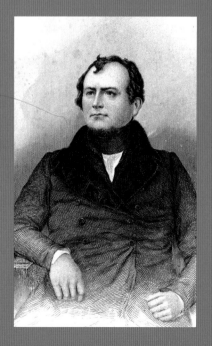

But his message had been heard. Thanks to Dorr's Rebellion, Rhode Island granted the vote to all adult males, both black and white, making it the only state where blacks and whites could vote as equals before the Civil War. Women, however, would have to wait another eighty years to win the right to vote.

THE BOMBARDMENT OF BRISTOL

On October 7, 1775, a small British fleet commanded by Captain James Wallace approached the seaside town of Bristol in search of supplies for the main fleet anchored in Newport Harbor. After a bombardment that lasted an hour and a half, Captain Wallace presented his demands: two hundred sheep and thirty cattle. After some negotiation, the matter was settled with the delivery of only forty sheep.

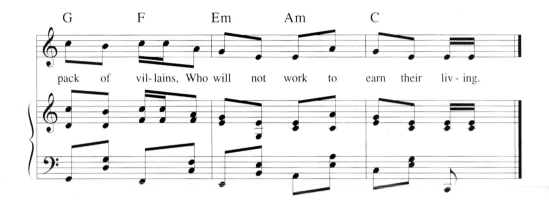

pack of vil-lains, Who will not work to earn their liv - ing.

In seventeen hundred and seventy-five
Our Bristol town was much surprised
By a pack of thievish villains,
That will not work to earn their livings.

October, 'twas the seventh day,
As I have heard the people say,
Wallace, his name be ever curst,
Came on our harbor just at dusk.

And there his ship did safely moor,
And quickly sent his barge on shore,
With orders that should not be broke,
Or they might expect a smoke.

Demanding that the magistrates
Should quickly come on board his ship,
And let him have some sheep and cattle,
Or that they might expect a battle.

At eight o'clock, by signal given,
Our peaceful atmosphere was riven
Women with Children in their arms,
With doleful cries ran to the farms.

With all their firing and their skill
They did not any person kill;
Neither was any person hurt
But the Reverend Parson Burt.

And he was not killed by a ball,
As judged by jurors one and all,
But being in a sickly state,
He, frightened, fell, which proved his fate.

Another truth to you I'll tell,
That you may see they leveled well,
For aiming for to kill the people,
They fired their shot into a steeple.

They fired low, they fired high,
The women scream, the children cry;
And all their firing and their racket
Shot off the topmast of a packet.

POPULATION GROWTH: 1790–2000

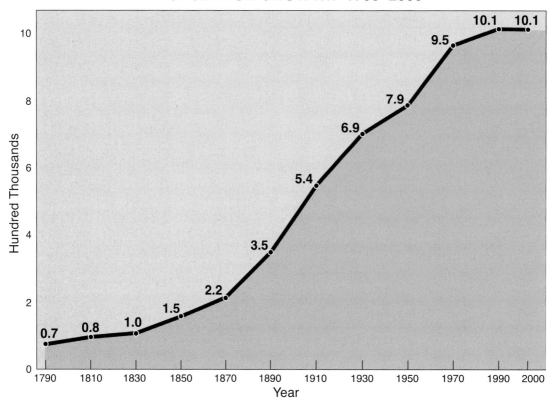

That same year, 1790, marked the birth of America's industrial revolution. The birthplace was Pawtucket, Rhode Island, where an English immigrant named Samuel Slater set up America's first successful water-powered cotton mill.

Slater, though a clever man, did not invent this process. That honor went to another Englishman, Sir Richard Arkwright, who had built a machine for spinning cotton into yarn. The English were so determined to keep the design to themselves that they passed laws preventing any crafts-people with knowledge of the machinery from leaving the country.

The first mechanical cotton mill (tall building in the center) was established by Samuel Slater in Pawtucket.

Of course, it is practically impossible to keep an idea from getting out. Slater had worked in one of Arkwright's mills for eight years and had carefully memorized the design. Dressed as a farmer, he had slipped out of the country illegally in 1789, knowing he could make his fortune.

By 1815 Rhode Island had one hundred cotton mills, and two-thirds of the state's villages had mills on their rivers. "The nation's Industrial Revolution was powered by *our* rivers," says journalist David Brussat. Rivers were dammed and reservoirs constructed to maintain a constant supply of water to turn the mill's waterwheels.

In Providence in 1827, Slater established the first steam-driven cotton mill. Soon steam power had replaced water power; factories could now be set up anywhere, not just on rivers, and they could operate year-round. By 1860 half the state's workers were employed in manufacturing, while only 10 percent worked on farms and 3 percent worked in fishing. Rhode Island had become the most industrialized state in the nation.

This was long before the era of child labor laws, and the majority of the mill workers were children, some as young as eight years old. Schooling became a remote possibility for these children once they joined the workforce. Most of the adult workers were women. Both women and children worked for lower wages than men.

Women and children worked in textile mills, working long hours and earning low wages.

The first half of the nineteenth century saw a growing division in America between the industrialized Northern states—which one by one outlawed slavery—and the Southern states, where wealthy landowners depended on slaves to work their fields. In late 1860—just after the election of Abraham Lincoln, who opposed the spread of slavery beyond the states where it already existed—South Carolina withdrew from the Union. It was followed in 1861 by ten more Southern states. Together, these states formed the Confederate States of America. The Civil War began in April 1861 when Confederate artillery fired on a federal fort in the Charleston, South Carolina, harbor. The war continued for four bloody years, taking the lives of more than 600,000 Americans on both sides.

As a center of industry, Rhode Island profited greatly from the war. Its factories worked overtime turning out cannons, rifles, and other weapons; its mills produced textiles for military uniforms, blankets, and tents. Patriotic feelings were strong—the state contributed 24,000 men to the Union cause, 5,000 more than the government requested.

After the war, another type of manufacturing gained importance in Providence: the metals industry. By 1900 the city was trumpeting its Five Industrial Wonders of the World, for within its borders stood the world's largest tool factory, file factory, steam engine factory, screw factory, and silverware factory. The city also became famous for its jewelry.

MODERN TIMES

By the early 1900s, Rhode Island's cotton mills were beginning to close, as businesses relocated to the South, where taxes were lower and labor was cheaper. Textiles remained the state's principal industry, but the boom years were over.

When the stock market crashed in 1929, millions of Americans were thrown out of work in the resulting Great Depression. But hard times had hit Rhode Island years earlier. Throughout the 1930s, mills continued to close. By 1937 nearly 80 percent of the Rhode Island cotton mills that had been operating in 1923 were gone.

With jobs scarce, people had to make do with less. Some found work at lower wages; others struggled to survive on part-time work. Many hungry Rhode Islanders depended on charities. Seafood—which was relatively cheap and plentiful in the Ocean State—became the staple diet for many Rhode Islanders. One woman recalled eating so many lobsters during these years that afterward she would never touch another one.

What pulled Rhode Island—and the rest of the United States—out of the Great Depression was World War II. As they had done during the Civil War, Rhode Island's industries produced goods that were needed for the war effort. But when the war ended in 1945, factories closed. More mills moved south.

Today, however, Rhode Island is prospering again. One reason for this is that the state's economy has diversified. Although manufacturing is still important, service industries, such as banking, insurance, and health care, have grown. Another reason for the prosperity in the state is the quality of life afforded in Rhode Island. As one historian wrote, "Life in Rhode Island is less hectic and more pleasant than in Boston or New York; and one is only minutes away from ocean beaches and forests." Rhode Island, which lost some of its population in the 1970s, is once again a place where people want to live.

It's also a place that people want to visit. Although it has always been a vacation spot because of its beaches, Rhode Island has learned

Rhode Island's history, culture, sights, and sounds contribute to the future of the state.

in recent decades to honor and preserve its past. Samuel Slater's cotton mill in Pawtucket is now a museum, and Providence has turned itself into a kind of living museum, with entire neighborhoods reflecting its colonial heritage. Throughout the state, there's a new understanding that one of Rhode Island's most valuable assets—the secret of its appeal and the source of its charm—is its history.

Chapter Three

A Million Rhode Islanders

It's easy to remember Rhode Island's size: just over 1,000 square miles. Its population is easy to remember, too: about one million people.

A SPECIAL PLACE

Despite their many differences, Rhode Islanders share a certain independent quality—an unwillingness to go along with the majority—that dates back to colonial days and may be a result of the state's small size. The publisher of the magazine *Rhode Island Monthly* speaks fondly of "our quirky but beloved little state," and journalists have celebrated the state's "eccentricity." Founded in part on tolerance, the city of Providence remains tolerant of people with unusual lifestyles, beliefs, and manners of dressing.

Yet, along with this sense of individuality and independence, in their dealings with people from other states, Rhode Islanders tend to display good-humored humility. "Living in a small state ensures that you will live

Rhode Islanders enjoy the gifts of the state and those who come to share it with them.

close to a border and increases the odds that you'll cross over it with more frequency than somebody living in, say, Montana," says the popular singer and songwriter Bill Harley, a former Rhode Island resident who now lives just across the border in Seekonk, Massachusetts. "People who live in Rhode Island . . . are border rats. We have a different view of the world." Because Rhode Islanders travel regularly to other states for bargains and jobs, they don't have inflated ideas of their own state's importance. They know they are just one part of a complex country, and that other, larger states are just a few miles down the highway. Despite their state's name, Rhode Islanders are never so arrogant as to think that they're living on an island.

Rhode Islanders celebrate their history during a summer parade.

ETHNIC RHODE ISLAND

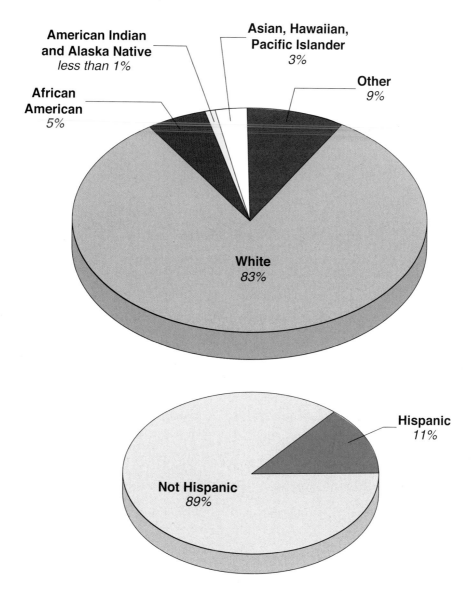

**American Indian
and Alaska Native**
less than 1%

**Asian, Hawaiian,
Pacific Islander**
3%

Other
9%

**African
American**
5%

White
83%

Hispanic
11%

Not Hispanic
89%

*Note: A person of Cuban, Mexican, Puerto Rican, South or Central American,
or other Spanish culture or origin, regardless of race, is defined as Hispanic.*

THE FIRST GREAT WAVES

Many states have been changed by immigration. Rhode Island has been totally transformed. It was first settled by immigrants from England who were seeking religious liberty, but in the mid-nineteenth century, Rhode Island's ethnic character began to change with the arrival of immigrants from Ireland. By 1880 nearly half the population of Providence was Irish-born or of Irish ancestry. The Irish continued to come to Rhode Island in large numbers through the 1930s.

Italians began to arrive in Rhode Island in the 1890s. By 1920 they outnumbered the immigrants from Ireland. Most Italians settled around Providence, particularly in the Federal Hill area, which they turned into a replica of their old home. In 1923 Providence writer H. P. Lovecraft described a visit to a restaurant "where only ourselves spoke English, and looking out into the bright street with the glittering Italian signs, we could only with difficulty believe that the main business section of Providence lay scarce a mile to the southeast." Italian Americans are now the largest ethnic group in Rhode Island (19 percent, according to census estimates for 2005), with Irish Americans just behind them (18.4 percent).

Other groups that brought special character to their Rhode Island neighborhoods are the French Canadians (17.3 percent) and the Portuguese (8.7 percent). French Canadians immigrated to Rhode Island in the late 1800s to work in mills in the northeast corner of the state. Many of them settled in Woonsocket on the Massachusetts border, turning it into what was called "the most French city in America," where, at the start of the twentieth century, French was spoken everywhere, even in the schools.

The Portuguese began arriving in Rhode Island around the same time. Some came from mainland Portugal, while many others arrived from Cape Verde and the Azores, rugged Portuguese islands in the Atlantic Ocean.

Rhode Island celebrates a Portuguese community of almost 9 percent.

The largest Portuguese community was in the Fox Point section of Providence. Until recent decades, this close-knit neighborhood had an almost foreign flavor. During the 1960s "you needed a passport to come to Fox Point," joked Harry Adler, whose family has run a hardware store there for three generations. "People talked about 'crossing the border' into the neighborhood."

Today, many people of Portuguese descent have left, and the neighborhood has transformed into one filled with gift shops, restaurants, and coffee bars. The old houses have become more expensive, and many are rented out to students from nearby Brown University. A Portuguese influence is still visible, however, in annual events such as the Cape Verdean Independence Day Festival each July, when India Point Park is filled with music and food from Cape Verde. Delicious Portuguese bread, as sweet as coffee cake, is popular throughout the state. Portuguese is still spoken in many homes in Rhode Island.

New immigrant groups continue to add to the variety that is Rhode Island. In recent years, Vietnamese, Cambodians, and people from the Dominican Republic and various African nations have settled in the state, seeking a better life. "You cannot tell Rhode Islanders that the American Dream doesn't work," historian William McLoughlin once said. "They have seen it work—not for all, but for enough; not always to the top, but a long way up, compared to life in the Old Country."

Because of the many immigrants from Ireland, Italy, French Canada, and Portugal, as well as Poles who settled in the Central Falls area, by 1910 the majority of Rhode Islanders were Roman Catholics. Since the 1950s a growing Hispanic population has added to the Catholic majority. Today 52 percent of Rhode Islanders are Catholic, making it the most Catholic state in the country. Some Rhode Islanders tend to think in terms of parishes, the area of their local church, rather than counties, towns, or neighborhoods. According to one Rhode Islander, during her childhood, "'out of parish' was as foreign as 'outtastate.'"

A Rhode Island couple partake in a traditional Loatian wedding ceremony.

THE TALK OF RHODE ISLAND

"One of the wonders of our state," a Rhode Island magazine once bragged, "is how a place so tiny can hold so many different accents."

"I love the way people here talk," says a South County man who returned to Rhode Island after living on the West Coast. "I've gotten to the point where I can differentiate between a Providence accent and a Newport accent." But although a native Rhode Islander may be able to pick out these regional differences, most outsiders hear a single, very distinctive way of speaking throughout the state.

All over the East Coast, many people drop the letter *r* in words, pronouncing it more like "ah." But in Rhode Island this tendency is often more extreme; sometimes *r* sounds like a cross between *w* and *v*. In a light-hearted study of Rhode Island speech, language expert Elaine Chaika offered these pronunciations:

area	*eahvia*	never	*neva*
bottle	*bah'il*	park	*pahk* or *pock*
farmer	*fahma*	parlor	*pala*
four	*faw*	partner	*potna*
here	*heah*	pure	*pyaw*
market	*mocket*	short	*shawt*

In his humorous *Rhode Island Dictionary*, Mark Patinkin adds that a Rhode Island auto mechanic may charge you for "pots and layba" (parts and labor), a Rhode Island lifeguard may warn you to be careful of the "shock" (shark), and a Rhode Island house may have a "coppit" (carpet) on the floor. Perhaps the most unforgettable of all Patinkin's terms is "P.S.D.S."—Rhode Islandese for "pierced ears."

THE JEWISH MIGRATIONS

Jews have lived in Rhode Island since colonial days. Like many other groups, they were attracted by the colony's religious tolerance. The first Jews in Rhode Island arrived in the 1650s. Settling mainly in Newport, they became tailors, merchants, candle makers, soap makers, and traders. There, in 1759, they began to build Touro Synagogue, the first synagogue in the colony. Still in use today, it is the oldest surviving Jewish house of worship in North America. In 1790, in a now-famous letter to the synagogue's congregation, President George Washington assured them of the new nation's commitment to religious liberty: "Happily the government of the United States . . . gives to bigotry no sanction, to persecution no assistance. . . . May the chil-

dren of the stock of Abraham who dwell in this land continue to merit and enjoy the good will of the other inhabitants, while every one shall sit in safety under his own vine and figtree, and there shall be none to make him afraid." Many more Jews arrived in Rhode Island in the 1880s and 1890s. They settled mainly in Providence, where they became shopkeepers or garment workers. Although Jews are a small segment of Rhode Island's population today, they are active in the arts, education, business, and politics.

Touro Synagogue, established in 1759, is the oldest synagogue in the United States.

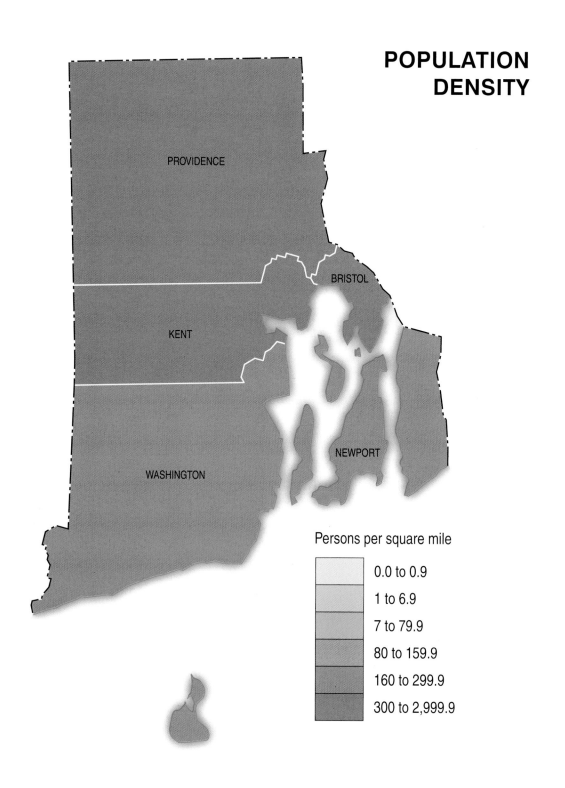

POPULATION DENSITY

Persons per square mile

	0.0 to 0.9
	1 to 6.9
	7 to 79.9
	80 to 159.9
	160 to 299.9
	300 to 2,999.9

PROVIDENCE

BRISTOL

KENT

NEWPORT

WASHINGTON

AFRICAN AMERICANS

African Americans, too, make up a relatively small part of the population—5 percent—and they, too, have been present in Rhode Island since colonial times. Before the American Revolution, most were slaves, but a few were free.

Though residents of Rhode Island since colonial days, African Americans make up only 5 percent of the population.

Slavery was dying out in Rhode Island by 1800, but freed African Americans were still treated as social outcasts. They were forced to use separate schools and churches, and they were banned from theaters, stagecoaches, and railroad cars. Many were harassed by rowdy whites. "If you were well dressed they would insult you for that, and if you were ragged you would surely be insulted for being so; be as peaceable as you could be, there was no shield for you," recalled William J. Brown, the descendant of slaves owned by Moses Brown, a leading Providence citizen.

The state's African-American population grew after the Civil War when they migrated to New England from the South. By the 1900s most African Americans in Rhode Island were transplanted Southerners, not the descendants of New England African Americans.

Today, Rhode Island's most prominent African American is Ruth J. Simmons, who in 2001 became the president of Brown University in Providence. Never before has an African American held so high a position at an Ivy League school. Simmons, whose academic focus was on French literature, grew up the twelfth child of poor sharecroppers in eastern Texas. Later, her father worked in a factory and her mother worked as a maid. They had little education, but as Simmons has written, they taught her the most important things she needed to know: "Their values

Ruth Simmons is the first African-American president of an Ivy League college.

were clear: do good work; don't ever get too big for your breeches; always be an authentic person; don't worry too much about being famous and rich because that doesn't amount to too much."

Many see a special meaning in the fact that Ruth Simmons—the great-great-granddaughter of slaves—is running a university whose early benefactors, including the Brown family, made some of their fortune from the slave trade. In 2004 she announced that she was setting up a committee of scholars—a Steering Committee on Slavery and Justice—to examine the role played by slave-trade money in the founding of the 240-year-old school—and to suggest possible ways that the school, if necessary, might make amends.

NATIVE AMERICANS TODAY

Most Rhode Islanders who describe themselves as Narragansett are probably also part African American, for during the nineteenth century, many members of the two groups intermarried. By 1833 few pure-blooded Narragansett remained. Most of them lived on a 9-square-mile reservation in Charlestown, along Rhode Island's southern coast, until 1880, when they sold the land to the state and the tribe was declared legally "extinct." In 1934 the Narragansett redeclared their tribal identity, and in 1978 some of their land was returned to them. Today, Native Americans make up around 0.5 percent of the state's population.

Many Native Americans gather each August for a Green Corn Thanksgiving on the grounds of Charlestown's Narragansett Indian Meeting House. This event is a two-day tribal meeting and powwow (a Narragansett word) with outdoor feasting, displays of Indian crafts, and dancing in traditional dress. The festival's sponsors claim that it is America's oldest annual event, dating back more than three hundred years.

Something else survives as well: dozens of Rhode Island towns and villages have Indian names, and so do some of the state's major rivers, such as the Pawtuxet, Sakonnet, Seekonk, Woonasquatucket, Moshassuck, and Pawcatuck.

Sachem Matthew Thomas is chief of the Narragansett Indian tribe.

JONNYCAKES

"We Rhode Islanders are almost religious about our jonnycakes," says a South County man. These celebrated pancakes—sometimes called "journey cakes" in colonial days (because they were a good food to take on journeys)—can be made from various kinds of cornmeal, but ideally you should use a rare type of stone-ground cornmeal called Rhode Island white cap flint corn, a strain that dates back to the Narragansett Indians and that is grown only in the southern part of the state. Have an adult help you with this recipe.

> 7 tablespoons of cornmeal
> 1 level tablespoon of sugar
> 1/2 teaspoon of salt
> 1/2 cup boiling water
> 1/2 cup of milk

Place the cornmeal, sugar, and salt in a bowl and pour boiling water over them to scald the meal. Beat the mixture to a smooth consistency, then beat in the milk.

Grease a heated griddle well, drop the batter by spoonfuls onto the griddle, and fry until the pancakes are golden brown on each side.

If you like your pancakes thin press each cake down firmly with a spatula. Thin jonnycakes—called "lacies" because of their ragged, lacy edges—are traditionally popular on the eastern side of Narragansett Bay. If you like them thick—as people do in the West Bay—do not press them at all.

Chapter Four

Power in the Smallest State

The center of Rhode Island's government is the beautiful white marble capitol in Providence. At the top of its dome stands an almost 12-foot bronze statue known as the Independent Man, a symbol of the Rhode Island spirit.

Providence was not always Rhode Island's only seat of government. Until 1854, Providence, Newport, East Greenwich, Bristol, and South Kingstown all served as capitals, and legislators traveled from one to the other so that no single region would be favored. No other state has ever had five capitals. In 1854 the number of capitals was reduced to two—Providence and Newport—and in 1900 Providence became the state's sole capital.

INSIDE GOVERNMENT

Rhode Island's government is modeled on the nation's, with three main divisions, each with its own power and responsibilities, and each serving to balance the others.

Rhode Island's State House houses the governor, lieutenant governor, secretary of state, treasurer, and the legislative branch of the government.

Executive

The head of the executive branch is the governor, who is elected to a four-year term. The governor prepares the state budget and accepts or rejects bills that are passed by the legislature. If the governor signs a bill, it becomes law. If he or she vetoes or rejects the bill, it does not.

Other important executive branch officials include the lieutenant governor, the secretary of state, the attorney general, and the general treasurer. These officials are elected independently, so it is possible for the governor and lieutenant governor to come from different political parties.

Rhode Island's fifty-seventh governor, Donald Carcieri, took office in January 2003.

Legislative

Like the U.S. Congress, Rhode Island's legislature—known as the General Assembly—is made up of a Senate and a House of Representatives. The thirty-eight senators and seventy-five representatives are all elected for two-year terms.

In the General Assembly, bills are introduced and voted on. If a bill passes, it goes to the governor for approval. If the governor vetoes it, a three-fifths majority in both houses can override the decision and turn the bill into law. The General Assembly also votes on whether to approve the budget that the governor proposes each year.

Rhode Island's House of Representatives in session after the opening of the General Assembly.

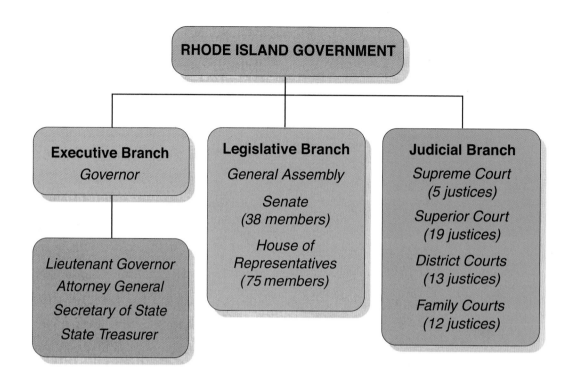

RHODE ISLAND GOVERNMENT

Executive Branch
Governor

Lieutenant Governor
Attorney General
Secretary of State
State Treasurer

Legislative Branch

General Assembly

Senate
(38 members)

House of
Representatives
(75 members)

Judicial Branch

Supreme Court
(5 justices)

Superior Court
(19 justices)

District Courts
(13 justices)

Family Courts
(12 justices)

Judicial

The judicial branch rules on legal matters and decides whether the other two branches have acted according to the law. Rhode Island's highest court, the state supreme court, has five justices who are appointed for life. Until 1994, these judges were chosen by the General Assembly—a system that invited corruption, since the legislature usually gave the jobs to fellow legislators. As a result, the judicial branch of government was not really independent of the legislative branch. Today, state supreme court justices are appointed by the governor, who selects from three to five candidates who are rated "highly qualified" by an independent commission. The choices must be approved by both chambers of the General Assembly.

The governor also appoints judges to five lower courts: the superior court and, below that, district, family, traffic, and workers' compensation courts. These appointments must be approved by the Senate.

Being a small state where people know one another has many advantages. A prominent Brown University history professor once remarked that Rhode Island was the only place he knew of where, if he chose, he could stroll down College Hill to the statehouse and probably have a chat with the governor without even making an appointment. When it comes to legal matters, however, the state's small size can be a problem, especially when one company or organization is suing another. As one *Providence Journal* reporter noted, "It can be difficult finding a judge who doesn't have a connection to someone involved in the lawsuit."

SHIFTING POWER

The twentieth century saw a great change in Rhode Island: a shift in political power from Republicans to Democrats, from old-line Yankee Protestants to newly arrived Catholic immigrants.

What is a Yankee? To someone from another country, a Yankee is anyone from the United States. To someone from a southern state, a Yankee is a northerner. But in the North itself, *Yankee* means a traditional New Englander whose ancestors came from England or Scotland.

Until the turn of the century, Rhode Island was controlled by the descendants of its early English settlers—by Yankees. They ran the businesses and newspapers, they had the most money, and they held most of the political offices. Most Yankees were staunch Republicans. But eventually, immigrants from countries, such as Ireland, Italy, Portugal, and France, began to outnumber this older segment of the population.

By the mid-1930s, the more recent arrivals and their descendants, who generally voted Democratic, were able to get elected to positions of power. Even though some Republicans have been elected governor, since 1935 Democrats have dominated Rhode Island politics and have never lost control of the General Assembly. Some people estimate that 85 percent of the votes in the assembly are nearly unanimous.

Today, judging by poll numbers, Rhode Island is probably the most heavily Democratic state in the country. In the 2000 presidential election it gave Al Gore his highest percentage of any state—61 percent—and in 2004 it gave John Kerry 59 percent, second only to his home state of Massachusetts. Rhode Island's registered Democrats outnumber Republicans by more than three to one.

POWER CORRUPTS

Decades of domination by one political party may lead to a sense of complacency and may invite corruption. When the Republicans controlled Rhode Island, they had been accused of vote-buying and other shady practices designed to enrich themselves and to maintain their political power. One late-nineteenth-century Republican politician, Charles "Boss" Brayton, famously declared that "an honest voter is one who stays bought." He argued that "the Democrats are just as bad—or would be, if they had the money." In fact, when the Democrats later took over, they were soon doing the same thing.

Until recently, Rhode Island was sometimes called the most corrupt state in the Union, and there was some truth to the charge. Bribery, misuse of funds, and the use of political office for personal gain were common. If you wanted to obtain a favor from a state senator, do business with a city, or influence the outcome of a trial, you paid a bribe. Since 1986 two chief justices of the Rhode Island Supreme Court have resigned in disgrace, and a superior court judge was arrested for taking a bribe. A particularly damaging scandal broke in 1990, when a prominent banker fled with $13 million from a bank that insured the funds in other banks. In the resulting scandal, forty-five banks and credit unions had to close temporarily, keeping more than 200,000 depositors from their accounts. Vincent A. "Buddy" Cianci Jr., the dynamic mayor of Providence, endured a series of scrapes with the law, including an assault conviction in 1984 that resulted in five years' probation, yet he was elected to office six times, making him the longest-serving big-city mayor in the country.

Providence's mayor Vincent Cianci Jr. is surrounded by the media after appearing in Federal court in 2001 on charges of racketeering and bribery.

Even though in 2002 he was sentenced to five years in federal prison for racketeering conspiracy, he remains a popular, even beloved figure among many Rhode Islanders. A Brown University professor said, "People take a perverse delight in chronicling the local corruption. It's part of the local entertainment."

What caused this corruption? Some point to the dominance of one political party, which has allowed legislators to ignore the law without fear of being voted out of office (although Cianci ran at various times as a Republican and as an Independent). Another factor has been the presence of organized crime. Until recently, the state was widely regarded as the New England headquarters of the Mafia. The state's small size has also contributed to the problem, by making it easier for friends to help one another evade the law.

H. Philip West, longtime executive director of Common Cause of Rhode Island, an organization dedicated to honesty in government, says that thanks to "massive public indignation" over recent scandals, the state has seen "profound changes that have been enacted with vast public support." In 1994, for example, 70 percent of voters approved the selection of all state judges based on merit. Today, said West, Rhode Island benefits from "radical new ethics laws and the strongest ethics commission in the United States. It has been a dramatic change, and it is working—not perfectly, but it is working."

LEARNING FROM DISASTER

Laws change slowly, often in response to terrible events. After enough fatalities, laws become stricter on drunken driving, and penalties become more severe. After a building collapses, a city introduces a stricter construction code. It sometimes takes a tragedy to get lawmakers moving.

RHODE ISLAND
BY COUNTY

PROVIDENCE

BRISTOL

KENT

NEWPORT

WASHINGTON

Remains in West Warwick are all that stand of The Station after a fire there that killed one hundred people in 2003.

Rhode Island was the scene of a tragedy on February 20, 2003, one that shocked the nation. A West Warwick nightclub called The Station was packed with spectators for a rock concert. One band's act featured fireworks, whose sparks accidentally set fire to soundproof foam panels with which the club had lined the walls because neighbors had complained about the noise. The foam was cheap and highly flammable. Within three minutes—perhaps even within 56 seconds—the club was an inferno filled with thick black smoke and deadly gas. One hundred people died.

In a state as small as Rhode Island, it seemed as if everyone knew at least one of the victims. The state mourned together like a single community. Over the next few years, a tough new fire code was put into effect that required nightclubs to install sprinkler systems and fire alarms connected to the nearest firehouse.

In 2006 the nightclub owner and the band manager received light prison sentences—just four years each. Grieving friends and family members were furious—"It's like a slap on the wrist," one said—but the judge stuck by his decision. "This criminal justice system," he explained, "cannot give you the relief you seek." That same year, the state opened a modern new disaster center in Cranston with links to all Rhode Island's thirty-nine cities and towns; it is designed for emergencies of all sorts, including hurricanes. The *Providence Journal* reported that today "Rhode Island is better prepared for a big fire."

Chapter Five
Wealth and Hard Work

Rhode Island is not especially rich in mineral resources. Although the state has some coal, its main minerals are limestone, granite, sand, and gravel, all of which are used in construction.

More important to the state is its fertile soil. Although housing has overtaken much of Rhode Island's farmland, potatoes, corn, and apples are still grown in the Narragansett Bay area. Barely two dozen dairy farms remain in the state (although there are now some llama farms), and only a few hundred people make their living from farming. In the spring of 2006, *Yankee* magazine profiled 80-year-old Charles Borders, who had spent his entire life working on his family's 200-acre farm in Foster, Rhode Island—"once a town full of farms," now down to just two. In a state that is "hungry for farmland," a place where farmers can make far more money by selling their land to developers than by continuing to farm, Borders, who has no children to whom he can leave his farm, had found a way to preserve the place he loved: by selling it to a group of nonprofit foundations that are pledged to keep the farm going after his death. "This is heaven on earth, right here," he said—and unlike most Rhode Island farmers, he knows it will remain that way.

The sea provides a source of income for Rhode Island and some of its residents.

Rhode Island's fertile ground provides acres of rich farmland.

The state bird, the hardy Rhode Island Red chicken, was raised in the 1850s near Adamsville. Today, the town has a granite marker proclaiming this fact—it is America's only monument to a chicken. No longer raised as widely as it once was, the bird is still popular among Rhode Islanders: "Loud, inbred, and confined to a small place, he is the perfect representative for our people," joked local writer Ted Widmer.

Rhode Islanders have long looked to the sea for prosperity from trade and fishing. The state continues to serve as a center for imports and exports, and much of New England's oil passes through the port of Providence. But only several hundred Rhode Islanders still make their living as fishermen, with hundreds more employed in other aspects of the fishing industry. The most common catches are lobster, cod, haddock, scrod, flounder, squid, hake, scup, whiting, butterfish, mackerel, and herring.

Rhode Island Red chickens have been raised in the state since the 1850s.

2005 GROSS STATE PRODUCT: $44 Million

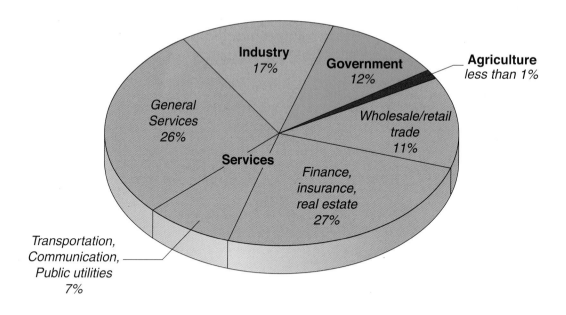

MANUFACTURING FOR THE NATION

Today, Rhode Island's economy relies on manufacturing. Although manufacturing remains a large source of jobs, it employs only around one-quarter of all Rhode Island workers, whereas fifty years ago it employed half.

Rhode Island factories produce electrical goods, precision tools, pens, luggage, furniture, glass, and various paper, chemical, plastic, leather, and rubber products. But the state's leading manufacturing industry is jewelry and silverware production. Rhode Island factories specialize in what is called costume jewelry—earrings, pins, watchbands, necklaces, and rings that are mass-produced and relatively low-priced. Providence used to proclaim itself "the jewelry capital of the world," and it has been estimated that 85 percent of the costume jewelry manufactured in the United States is made in the Providence area.

Rhode Island's primary manufacturing industries are jewelry (above) and silverware.

That sounds impressive, but in truth, the industry has been hurt in recent years. Increasingly, costume jewelry is being imported from China and other Asian nations, where it can be manufactured at a fraction of the cost. Some Chinese factories are counterfeiting Rhode Island-made jewelry, including the brand names, flooding the U.S. market with cheap imitations that people mistake for the genuine product. As a result, most Rhode Island jewelry factories have closed, and others are struggling to survive. "Several years ago a major American company offered to buy 100,000 corporate medallions from me if

I could match, or even come close to, the unit prices they cost in Taiwan: twelve to fourteen cents each," said a retired Rhode Island jewelry executive. "I contacted nearly a dozen firms in Providence, and the cheapest price they could quote me was twenty-eight cents." The inability to compete, he says, is the Rhode Island jewelry industry's largest problem. In 2005 an executive from one of Providence's few remaining costume-jewelry factories toured the Hong Kong show-rooms of China's growing jewelry industry and reached the same conclusion: "There was nothing we could make in the U.S. that couldn't be made far less expensively in China." Later that year, the Providence factory closed.

One of Rhode Island's great success stories has been the Hasbro toy company, the second-largest toymaker in the world, which has its headquarters in Pawtucket. Hasbro is short for the *Has*senfeld *bro*thers, Henry and Halel, immigrants from Eastern Europe who, in 1924, opened a shop in Providence selling textile remnants—leftover pieces of cloth. They began to turn some of their remnants into cloth-covered pencil boxes. Later the company manufactured toy doctor's and nurse's kits. Hasbro hit the big time in 1952 with Mr. Potato Head, the first toy ever advertised on television, and the company now makes many of America's favorite playthings, including Raggedy Ann, Spirograph, Tinkertoys, Tonka Trucks, G.I. Joe, Lincoln Logs, Play-Doh, Nerf, games such as Scrabble, Monopoly, and Clue, and an ever-growing number of *Star Wars* and Marvel superhero toys. Still a family-run business with $3 billion in annual sales, Hasbro employs ten thousand people around the world. In 1994 the company established the Hasbro Children's Hospital in Providence, the largest and most advanced facility of its kind in the state.

Hasbro shows off its toys at the 2005 International Toy Fair in New York City.

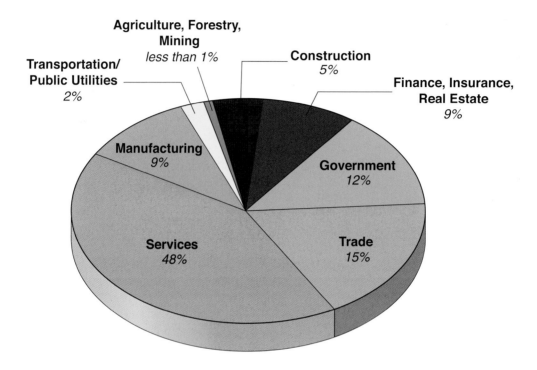

RHODE ISLAND WORKFORCE

Agriculture, Forestry, Mining
less than 1%

Transportation/ Public Utilities
2%

Construction
5%

Finance, Insurance, Real Estate
9%

Manufacturing
9%

Government
12%

Services
48%

Trade
15%

THE SERVICE ECONOMY

Over the past half century, the service industry has become increasingly important to Rhode Island's economy. Today, in fact, the most common jobs in Rhode Island are in two service industries, tourism and health care. A dozen of the one hundred largest private employers in the state are hospitals and health-related agencies. Education plays a major role as well. Brown University is the state's seventh-largest private employer. Tourism brings more than $1.6 billion yearly to Rhode Island and supports over 25,000 jobs. "If it weren't for tourists, I wouldn't survive," says a Providence bookseller.

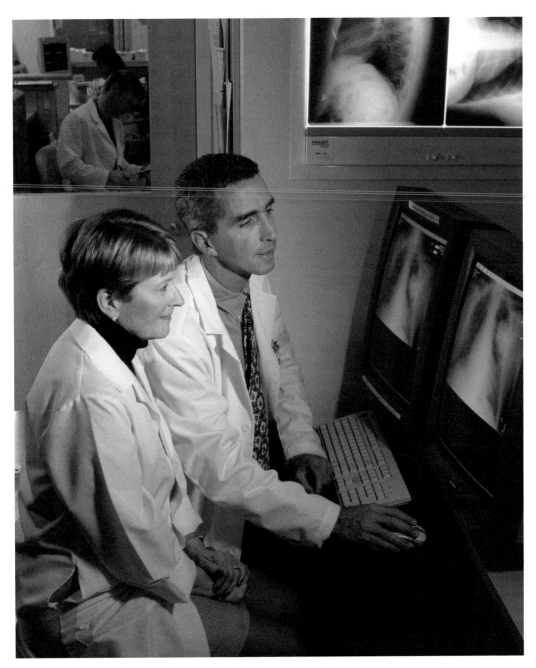

Health care employs a large sector of the state's residents.

NIGHT OWLS

Anyone who has ever eaten in an all-night diner owes thanks to Walter Scott, who invented this most American of restaurants in Providence in 1872. Aware that most restaurants closed at 8:00 P.M., Scott loaded a horse-drawn wagon with pies, sandwiches, and coffee to sell to hungry workers on the night shift. The idea caught on all over New England, and wagons like Scott's, known as "night owls," were soon serving other sorts of food as well, including hot dogs, beans, and cold cuts. By 1880 there were thirty wagons in Providence alone, and by 1917 there were fifty.

In the twentieth century, night owls became motorized, and later, instead of traveling to their customers, they became stationary, like other restaurants. They began to resemble streamlined railroad cars, like the beautiful Modern Diner (above) in Pawtucket, Rhode Island, the first diner ever listed in the National Register of Historic Places. But in Providence, the diner's birthplace—where a diner museum is in the works—a beloved night owl called Haven Brothers still motors through downtown every afternoon at 4:30 P.M. and parks near city hall, serving franks and beans to hungry Rhode Islanders before disappearing at dawn.

EARNING A LIVING

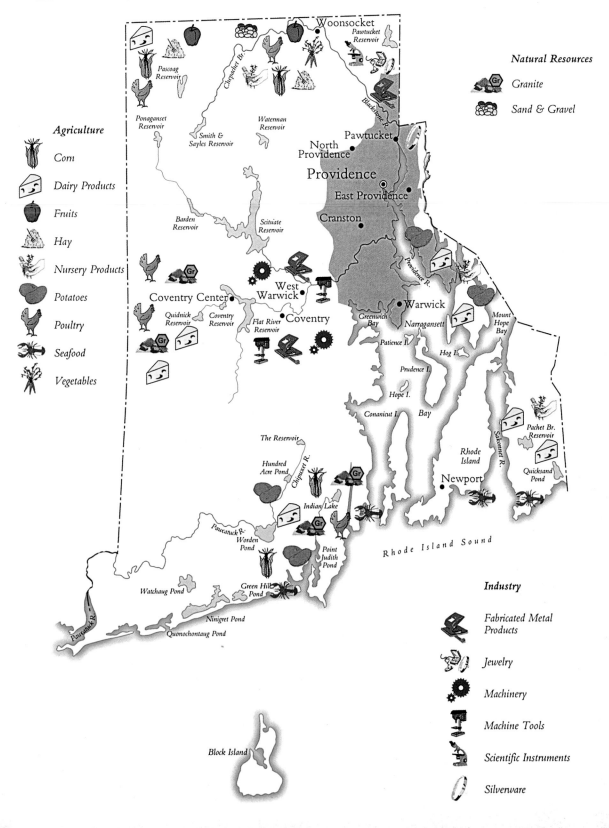

Natural Resources

Granite

Sand & Gravel

Agriculture

Corn

Dairy Products

Fruits

Hay

Nursery Products

Potatoes

Poultry

Seafood

Vegetables

Industry

Fabricated Metal Products

Jewelry

Machinery

Machine Tools

Scientific Instruments

Silverware

Woonsocket
Pawtucket Reservoir
Pascoag Reservoir
Chepachet Br.
Waterman Reservoir
Ponaganset Reservoir
Smith & Sayles Reservoir
Blackstone R.
North Providence
Pawtucket
Providence
East Providence
Cranston
Barden Reservoir
Scituate Reservoir
Coventry Center
West Warwick
Warwick
Quidnick Reservoir
Coventry Reservoir
Flat River Reservoir
Coventry
Greenwich Bay
Narragansett
Mount Hope Bay
Providence R.
Patience I.
Hog I.
Prudence I.
Hope I.
Conanicut I.
Bay
The Reservoir
Hundred Acre Pond
Chipuxet R.
Indian Lake
Rhode Island
Newport
Sakonnet R.
Pachet Br. Reservoir
Quicksand Pond
Pawcatuck R.
Worden Pond
Point Judith Pond
Rhode Island Sound
Watchaug Pond
Green Hill Pond
Ninigret Pond
Quonochontaug Pond
Pawcatuck R.

Block Island

Companies in service industries such as banking and insurance have relocated to Rhode Island because the cost of doing business is lower there than in major metropolitan areas such as Boston, as is the cost of living for employees. Providence, in particular, is viewed as a good place to start a business. "It's between New York and Boston," explains one executive, "so we are near the international financial centers, but we are not burdened by the choking influence of a large city."

GRADING EDUCATION

One key to competing economically with other states—and to attracting both businesses and individuals—is the quality of public education. Rhode Island's record in this area reveals some odd strengths and weaknesses. One 2005 survey ranked Rhode Island's eighth-graders thirty-eighth among the states in math skills, and its average SAT scores rank the state forty-third. However, the percentage of Rhode Island students who take the SATs is nearly twice the national average—and that may explain the low scores. The state's most important newspaper, the *Providence Journal*, has been critical of public education in the state: "Teachers' pay ranks sixth or seventh in America," an editorial said, "but Rhode Island students consistently rank near the bottom regionally in test scores."

Rhode Island taxpayers worry about whether they are getting their money's worth in education, and many parents are concerned about misbehavior in the classroom. They want schools to get tough with troublemakers who disrupt the class. And they are very keen—more so than most Americans—on community service as a part of education. "It gets the kids involved in the community, it gives them something to do, and it gives them something to be proud of," said a mother with a son and daughter in school. "For some kids, it might be the only thing they can do that they feel good about, confident about. I feel strongly about community service."

But some Rhode Islanders—including Gary Sasse, a prominent businessman and advisor to the governor—worry about whether Rhode Island students will be strong enough to compete in the world economy.

Rhode Island's Department of Elementary and Secondary Education commissioner Peter McWalters stated, "Let's work together to ensure the best possible public education for all our students."

Chapter Six

Rhode Island Highlights

Visiting Rhode Island is a treat. As *Yankee* magazine suggested, "Here is a state to explore in a weekend on a single tank of gas." There aren't any majestic mountains, vast prairies, or scenic vistas, but the state is friendly and comfortable, traveling is easy, and the food—especially Italian food and seafood—is delicious. With its beautiful beaches and nature preserves, Rhode Island is a fine state for people who enjoy swimming, fishing, boating, and bird-watching. And for anyone who loves charming architecture and a sense of the past, it's unbeatable.

PROVIDENCE

Rhode Island has sometimes been described as a city-state because it is so dominated by Providence, New England's second-largest city. The entire state can be seen as a suburb of Providence; no matter where you live in the state (except for Block Island), you can commute to work in Providence in less than an hour. According to former Rhode Islanders Walter and Hazel Knof, when people speak of "going downtown," they mean going to Providence.

Rhode Island's shores are a big draw to the state.

93

Providence is a city offering its visitors culture and history.

As one of America's oldest cities, Providence has had its ups and downs. A prosperous seaport in colonial days, it became a center of commerce and industry in the nineteenth century. By the middle of the twentieth century, its once-fashionable stores were closing and businesses were leaving. Today, after decades of decline, it is thriving again.

Recent years have seen monumental changes in the city's very shape. New shopping areas have been constructed, including an elegantly designed mall called Providence Place, and the city's downtown now features a new Rhode Island Convention Center, an ice-skating rink, and a handsome new train station. The old railroad tracks have been rerouted, and so has the Providence River, which had long been covered over by roadways. Visible once again and spanned by a dozen new bridges in a massive effort to revitalize and beautify the city, the river flows in a graceful curve past the downtown business district and the state capitol. In Waterplace Park by the river, you can take rides in narrow boats called gondolas or, on summer nights, enjoy shows in the amphitheater.

These changes have excited longtime residents as well as visitors. As a writer in *Rhode Island Monthly* put it: "This is a state that moves rivers, for crying out loud, if that's what it takes to make its capital city beautiful and vital again."

Thanks to the reemergence of the Providence River, visitors can also enjoy an outdoor nighttime event—once unique to this city but now imitated elsewhere—called WaterFire, in which, from sunset till midnight, as many as one hundred bonfires are set alight on special platforms in the middle of the river, illuminating the water for more than half a mile, accompanied by atmospheric music. Described as "a powerful work of art and a moving symbol of Providence's renaissance," the event is held several times a month from May through

Spectators watch WaterFire along the Providence River.

October and, since its beginning in 1994, has proved immensely popular. Its organizers have said: "WaterFire's sparkling bonfires, the fragrant scent of aromatic wood smoke, the flickering firelight on the arched bridges, the silhouettes of the firetenders passing by the flames, the torch-lit vessels traveling down the river, and the enchanting music from across the world all engage the senses and emotions of those who stroll the paths and bridges of Waterplace Park."

In other parts of town, money has been spent not on changing the old look of the city, but on preserving it. One downtown landmark that has been preserved is the Arcade, a majestic three-story building. When it was completed in 1828, it was revolutionary—America's first indoor shopping mall.

Its huge granite pillars, each weighing more than 12 tons, were hauled one by one from a quarry in Johnston, Rhode Island, by a team of fifteen oxen. Today the Arcade is owned by Johnson & Wales University, which offers degrees in restaurant management and cooking, but the old building is still filled with shops and cafés, much as it was over 150 years ago.

Colleges have come to the rescue of other Providence landmarks as well. At the foot of College Hill, the Old Stone Bank building, known for its ornate gold dome, has been bought by Brown University. "Nothing around here gets wasted," said Fox Point resident Abby Sheckley. "They used to tear old buildings down, but now they're trying to save them."

Midway up College Hill lies beautiful Benefit Street, first laid out in 1758. Visitors are treated to "A Mile of History," passing through a neighborhood that contains more colonial and early-nineteenth-century houses than can be found anywhere else in America. The modern electric streetlights that once lined its sidewalks have been replaced by old-fashioned flickering gas lamps. Each June a selection of old homes in Providence—including those in the Benefit Street area—are opened to the public during the Festival of Historic Houses, which never fails to attract large crowds.

Benefit Street in Providence is part of the state's National historic district.

One Benefit Street house that's always open to the public is the John Brown House, an impressive brick building that dates back to 1786. Inside are rooms furnished just as they were in the eighteenth century and decorated with reproductions of original wallpaper. On display are fine china plates and bowls that are actually *from* China, brought back in John Brown's ships, which were the first from Rhode Island to trade with that country in the years following the American Revolution. There is also a collection of antique dolls and toys.

John Brown was the wealthiest member of the famous Brown family. He and his brothers Joseph, Nicholas, and Moses were Providence's most important citizens in the late 1700s. It was Joseph who designed John's house, and he must have done a good job, because President John Quincy Adams, when he visited Providence as a boy, praised it as one of the "most magnificent and elegant mansions that I have ever seen on this continent." Joseph Brown also served as architect for America's oldest Baptist church, built in 1775. Crowned by a graceful 185-foot spire, the church stands just off Benefit Street, six blocks from the Brown mansion.

Brown University, named after Nicholas Brown Jr., and the neighboring Rhode Island School of Design, a leading art school, dominate College Hill in Providence. Founded in 1764, Brown is America's seventh-oldest college, and it attracts top students from around the world. Brown's oldest building, University Hall, is a handsome red-brick structure crowned by a bell tower. According to newspaper columnist Anne Allinson, it is a building "whose architecture transmits the dignity and grace of colonial days."

Also on College Hill is peaceful Prospect Terrace, where a 14-foot statue of Roger Williams stands overlooking the city that he founded, his right hand raised in blessing. Beneath the statue is buried what is left of Williams's body—now a handful of dust.

Providence is home to one of the nation's top schools, Brown University.

PRESERVING THE PAST

Visitors to Rhode Island will find a wealth of eighteenth- and nineteenth-century houses that no other state can match—"a collection of beautiful architecture so vast," said writer Nathaniel Reade, "it's like a three-dimensional architectural textbook."

Things weren't always this way. By the late 1940s many old homes—including some on Providence's Benefit Street—were so shabby and run-down that they were slated to be demolished. Many were supposed to be replaced by a highway.

Concerned about the state of their city, a group of prominent citizens founded the Providence Preservation Society in 1956, and architectural historian Antoinette Downing educated Rhode Islanders about the rich architectural heritage they were about to lose. She convinced the city to sell abandoned homes cheaply to young people who were capable of renovating them, and she raised money to help with the repair work.

In Newport, multimillionaire heiress Doris Duke formed the Newport Restoration Foundation in 1968 to restore that town's colonial houses, and Katherine Urquhart Warren founded the Preservation Society of Newport County, convincing wealthy members of the community to support the maintenance of Newport's fabulous mansions. "Money is no object at all," she once said. "I could raise $100,000 or $200,000 over the lunch table any day of the week."

Thanks to these dedicated people, the past is still alive in Rhode Island.

TEN LARGEST CITIES

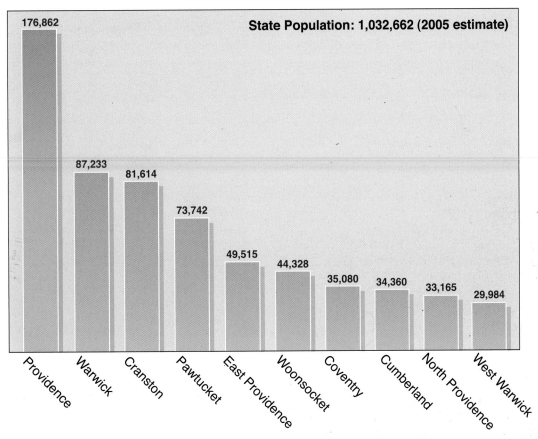

State Population: 1,032,662 (2005 estimate)

- Providence: 176,862
- Warwick: 87,233
- Cranston: 81,614
- Pawtucket: 73,742
- East Providence: 49,515
- Woonsocket: 44,328
- Coventry: 35,080
- Cumberland: 34,360
- North Providence: 33,165
- West Warwick: 29,984

NEWPORT

Newport, Rhode Island is known as "America's First Resort." It has come to stand for entertainment, sports, high society, beaches, and, in a word, *fun*.

Mention Newport to music lovers and they will likely think of its world-renowned summertime folk, jazz, and classical music festivals. Dozens of the most famous names in music have played there, from internationally acclaimed pianists to Louis Armstrong, Bob Dylan, Johnny Cash, and the

Indigo Girls. "A mellow crowd lazed on their chaises and quilts," one happy concertgoer recalled, "reading the Sunday paper, drinking lemonade, eating ice cream. I never saw the sun so bright, the skies so blue, the sails in Newport harbor so white. And during lulls, we could hear the waves crashing on the shore."

Newport is well known as the sailing capital of America.

Mention Newport to architecture lovers and they'll think of the more than five hundred colonial-era houses still found there—more than in any other city in America. But Newport is even better known as the place where, in the nineteenth century, the rich built their summer homes, enormous and opulent mansions that the owners jokingly referred to as "cottages." Wealthy southern landowners first began to summer in Newport in the eighteenth century. The first of the celebrated cottages was Kingscote, built for a Georgia plantation owner in 1839. Today it is a museum, and its elaborately decorated rooms, stained-glass windows, and expensive furnishings are open to the public.

An even grander mansion is Belcourt Castle, a sixty-room home built for just one man, a thirty-six-year-old bachelor named Oliver Hazard Perry Belmont. Three hundred craftsmen were brought over from Europe to work on it. The banquet hall can seat 250 people for dinner and 500 for concerts. Highlights of a visit to Belcourt Castle include a reproduction of an ornate royal Portuguese coronation coach and a grand ballroom with stained-glass windows.

Some of these lavish estates border Rhode Island Sound and can be seen if you take the Cliff Walk, a three-mile-long footpath that winds along the rocky coast between the backyards of these mansions and the sea.

Coastal strolls along Cliff Walk showcase the mansions of the gilded age.

Those who love beautiful landscaping will enjoy an unusual nineteenth-century garden in nearby Portsmouth. Green Animals, as it's called, is a topiary garden, in which shrubs and trees are carefully clipped into familiar shapes. There are eighty such sculptures here, including twenty-one of animals. There are also greenhouses, flower beds, and a Victorian toy collection.

Newport is also called the Yachting Capital of the World. From 1930 to 1983 the waters off Newport were the U.S. site of the America's Cup race, an international competition that is the World Series of sailing. In Newport, you can take lessons in everything from sailing and windsurfing to boat repair and kayaking, or set sail on a guided cruise around the Aquidneck coast. You can also visit a replica of the *Providence*, a sailing ship that fought in the American Revolution.

As you might expect, Newport has several lighthouses to help ships navigate safely. Especially well known is the one at Lime Rock, which is no longer active. In the 1800s the lighthouse keeper's daughter, Ida Lewis, became known as "the greatest saltwater heroine in American history" because she saved as many as twenty-five people from drowning—rescuing the first when she was just seventeen years old—often rowing out alone onto stormy seas with a rescue line to save boaters. The citizens of Newport rewarded her bravery with a new rowboat called the *Rescue*. It was made of mahogany and had gold-plated oarlocks and red velvet cushions.

Sailboats take part in the America's Cup off Newport.

PLACES TO SEE

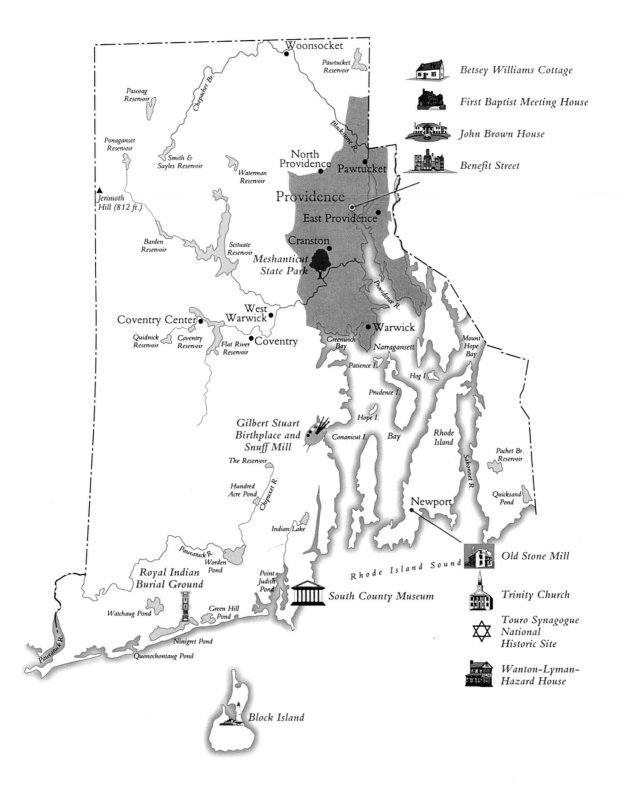

Betsey Williams Cottage

First Baptist Meeting House

John Brown House

Benefit Street

Woonsocket

Pawtucket Reservoir

Pascoag Reservoir

Chepachet Br.

Blackstone R.

Ponaganset Reservoir

North Providence

Pawtucket

Smith & Sayles Reservoir

Waterman Reservoir

Jerimoth Hill (812 ft.)

Providence

East Providence

Barden Reservoir

Scituate Reservoir

Cranston

Meshanticut State Park

Providence R.

West Warwick

Coventry Center

Warwick

Quidnick Reservoir

Coventry Reservoir

Flat River Reservoir

Coventry

Greenwich Bay

Narragansett

Mount Hope Bay

Patience I.

Hog I.

Prudence I.

Gilbert Stuart Birthplace and Snuff Mill

Hope I.

Conanicut I.

Bay

Rhode Island

Pachet Br. Reservoir

The Reservoir

Sakonnet R.

Quicksand Pond

Hundred Acre Pond

Chipuxet R.

Newport

Old Stone Mill

Indian Lake

Rhode Island Sound

Pawcatuck R.

Worden Pond

Trinity Church

Royal Indian Burial Ground

Point Judith Pond

South County Museum

Touro Synagogue National Historic Site

Watchaug Pond

Green Hill Pond

Pawcatuck R.

Ninigret Pond

Wanton-Lyman-Hazard House

Quonochontaug Pond

Block Island

BLOCK ISLAND

Vacationers in the 1890s called Block Island the Bermuda of the North. Today, although there are a lot more tourists and summer homes, it's still a special place of windswept dunes, low hills covered with beach grass, and views of the ocean from one's bedroom. "Block Island has the most sensational countryside of all of Rhode Island's islands," said writer Pamela Petro. "It's also the most crowded."

Block Island has been called "One of the Last Twelve Great Places in the Western Hemisphere."

There isn't a lot to do on Block Island but relax, read, fish, or go for a ride on a rented bicycle or motor scooter. Visitors seem to like it that way; many of them come back summer after summer. There's one other pastime for visitors: searching for pirate gold. America's first naval battle took place off the island in 1690 when a pirate named Thomas Paine, with two boats, fired on a small fleet of vessels commanded by a French pirate, Captain Picard. It's believed that one of the most infamous pirates of all, Captain William Kidd, may have buried treasure here.

SOUTH COUNTY AND BEYOND

Except for the trip to Block Island, traveling in the Ocean State is not much of a chore. The state is so small that drives are not tiring, and the Claiborne Pell Newport, Mount Hope, and Jamestown-Verrazzano Bridges—three of New England's longest bridges—span Narragansett Bay, connecting its largest islands to the mainland. (The last of these bridges replaced the Jamestown Bridge, which opened in 1940 and was closed in 1992. In April 2006 the old bridge—described as an eyesore—was demolished with the first of a series of controlled explosions while hundreds of observers on shore and in boats watched the event; others watched on a local cable TV station or online on their computers.)

Still, some Rhode Islanders are happiest staying close to home. In one of Don Bousquet's cartoons, a backwoodsman with an ax finds himself face-to-face with a little space alien holding a ray-gun. "You want to abduct *me*??" the Rhode Islander says with amazement. "Listen, pal, I'm from South County and I never even go as far as Providence!"

South County is what Rhode Islanders call Kent County and Washington County, the state's southern portion, west of Narragansett

Claiborne Pell Bridge connects Rhode Island and Connecticut.

Bay, and it's true that you can have a fine time without leaving the area, especially in the summer. Beaches such as East Matunuck, Misquamicut, Scarborough, and Narragansett attract thousands of visitors. Nature preserves such as Ninigret Pond and Trustom Pond, with their mixture of open spaces and trees, attract migrating birds such as gulls, terns, sandpipers, and ducks, and songbirds such as warblers, robins, catbirds, and flickers—as well as scores of dedicated bird-watchers.

One of the most charming spots in the state is Watch Hill at the southwestern tip of Rhode Island, a little seaside town with a few old hotels and handsome, often grand summer homes. It also has a beautiful beach with a lighthouse built in 1856 (it is closed to the public), a harbor filled with pleasure boats, a single street of old-fashioned shops and restaurants, and what is considered to be America's oldest merry-go-round still in operation, the Flying Horse Carousel, built sometime between 1850 and 1883 (no one knows exactly when), with hand-carved wooden horses.

Bristol, on the eastern side of Narragansett Bay, is noted for its lavish Fourth of July parade, one of the nation's largest, which also claims to be the oldest. In August comes another celebration, the two-day Quahog Festival in North Kingstown, on the western shore of the bay, where seafood of all sorts, but most notably Rhode Island's favorite clam, is downed by hungry visitors. North Kingstown's special pride is the prosperous harbor village of Wickford, which is filled with well-maintained houses from centuries past. As one contented resident said, "It is a place where time seems to have stopped in the 1820s." In short, it's like the state of Rhode Island itself—a place where the charm and beauty of the past is honored and preserved.

THE FLAG: The flag's white background symbolizes soldiers who lost their lives during the American Revolution. A gold anchor in the center of the flag represents hope and is surrounded by thirteen gold stars that symbolize the thirteen original colonies. Under the anchor is a blue ribbon on which is inscribed the word Hope, the state motto, in gold letters. The flag was adopted in 1897.

THE SEAL: A gold anchor similar to the one on the state flag appears in the center of the seal. The word Hope is inscribed above the anchor. At the bottom of the border that surrounds the inner part of the seal is "1636," the year Roger Williams established Providence, Rhode Island's first permanent European settlement. The state seal was adopted in 1896.

State Survey

Statehood: May 29, 1790

Origin of Name: Dutch explorer Adriaen Block called it *roodt eylandt*, meaning "red island," because of its red clay. Italian explorer Giovanni da Verrazano compared the local islands to the Greek island of Rhodes.

Nickname: Ocean State

Capital: Providence

Motto: Hope

Bird: Rhode Island Red chicken

Flower: Violet

Tree: Red maple

Stone: Cumberlandite

Mineral: Bowenite

Violet

RHODE ISLAND'S IT FOR ME

Charlie Hall, who wrote the lyrics to Rhode Island's state song, created a comedy cabaret in 1992 called *Ocean State Follies*, which poked good-natured fun at Rhode Island celebrities and politicians. When challenged to write a positive song about the state, Hall came up with a set of lyrics inspired by the state's natural beauty. Maria Day, a cast member of the *Follies*, wrote the melody. The song was adopted as the official state song in 1996.

Lyrics by Charlie Hall   **Music by Maria Day**

GEOGRAPHY

Highest Point: 812 feet, at Jerimoth Hill

Lowest Point: sea level, along the Atlantic coast

Area: 1,214 square miles

Greatest Distance North to South: 48 miles

Greatest Distance East to West: 37 miles

Bordering States: Connecticut on the west, Massachusetts to the north and east

Hottest Recorded Temperature: 104º F at Providence on August 2, 1975

Coldest Recorded Temperature: –25º F at Greene, Rhode Island on February 5, 1996

Average Annual Precipitation: 44 inches

Major Rivers: Blackstone, Moshassuck, Pawcatuck, Pawtuxet, Providence, Seekonk

Major Lakes: Flat River Reservoir, Pascoag Lake, Scituate Reservoir, Smith and Sayles Reservoir, Worden Pond

Trees: ash, beech, birch, cedar, dogwood, elm, hemlock, hickory, maple, oak, pine, poplar, willow

Wild Plants: aster, buttercup, cattail, daisy, fern, goldenrod, lily, scarlet pimpernel, rhododendron, seaweed, swamp azalea, trillium, violet, wild carrot, wild rose

Animals: beaver, fox, coyote, hare, mink, mole, muskrat, opossum, otter, rabbit, raccoon, squirrel, white-tailed deer, woodchuck

Raccoon

Birds: barred owl, blue jay, cardinal, catbird, chickadee, crow, dove, duck, eagle, flicker, hawk, osprey, partridge, pigeon, robin, sparrow, tern, woodpecker, wren

Fish: bluefin tuna, bluefish, cod, eel, flounder, mackerel, perch, pike, sea bass, shark, striped bass, swordfish, trout

Shellfish: blue crab, lobster, mussel, oyster, quahog, scallop, soft-shell clam

Endangered Animals: American burying beetle, Atlantic leatherback turtle, Atlantic sea turtle, piping plover, roseate tern

Tern

TIMELINE

c. 1400 Narragansett and Wampanoag Indians live in present-day Rhode Island.

1524 Italian navigator Giovanni da Verrazano explores Narragansett Bay.

1614 Dutch navigator Adriaen Block lands on what is later named Block Island.

1636 Roger Williams establishes Providence.

1638 William Coddington, John Clarke, Anne Hutchinson, and others found Portsmouth.

1639 Roger Williams and Ezekiel Holliman found America's first Baptist church, the Baptist Society of America, in Providence.

1644 Roger Williams obtains a charter from England for the Rhode Island colony.

1663 King Charles II grants Rhode Island a second charter, which provides for religious freedom and self-governance.

1699 Quakers in Newport set up the colony's first Quaker meetinghouse.

1739 Spaniards seize smuggler Robert Jenkins's ship and cut off his ear, thus beginning the War of Jenkins's Ear, or King George's War.

1764 Rhode Island College, which later becomes Brown University, is founded.

1776 Two months before signing the Declaration of Independence, Rhode Island becomes first colony to renounce its allegiance to England.

1790 Rhode Island becomes the thirteenth state.

1835 Rhode Island's first railroad begins operation between Providence and Boston.

1842 Thomas Dorr leads a reform movement known as Dorr's Rebellion, which demands voting rights for all adult white males.

1882 Public education become mandatory.

1883 U.S. Navy opens Newport Naval Station.

1900 Providence becomes Rhode Island's sole capital.

1938 A severe hurricane results in 317 deaths and $100 million in property damage.

1954 First U.S. jazz festival held in Newport.

1969 Rhode Island's sector of Interstate 95 is completed; Claiborne Pell Newport Bridge over Narragansett Bay opens.

1971 State personal income tax is approved.

1973 U.S. Navy shuts down Quonset Point Naval Air Station.

1990 Rhode Island celebrates its two-hundredth anniversary of statehood.

1991 The Crandall family of Westerly, unable to afford the taxes on their 350-acre farm valued at over $1 million, relinquishes the farm to the Narragansett Indians after 332 years of ownership.

1992 Voters pass an amendment lengthening the governor's term of office from two years to four—the prevailing term for all but three states.

1996 A tank barge runs aground at Moonstone Beach, spilling 828,000 gallons of home heating oil into Block Island Sound and devastating local bird and marine life.

1999 Providence opens a major new shopping mall containing 160 stores, in downtown Providence.

2001 Ruth J. Simmons becomes president of Brown University, the first African American to head an Ivy League college.

2003 A fire at a rock concert in a West Warwick nightclub kills 100 people.

2004 Rhode Island leads the New England States in job growth.

2006 Lincoln Chafee, regarded as the U.S. Senate's most liberal Republican, loses his seat in a national Democratic sweep to former Rhode Island attorney general Sheldon Whitehouse.

ECONOMY

Agricultural Products: apples, dairy products, hay, potatoes, poultry, snap beans, squash, sweet corn

Manufactured Products: appliances, boats and ships, electrical equipment, farm machinery, jewelry, metal products, printed materials, rubber products, silverware

Jewelry

Natural Resources: coal, granite, graphite, iron, limestone, and sandstone

Business and Trade: communications, finance, insurance, real estate, retail trade, transportation, wholesale trade

CALENDAR OF CELEBRATIONS

Polar Bear Plunge The hearty welcome New Year's Day the hard way, when members of the Newport Polar Bear Club, who swim outdoors year-round, are joined by amateurs and spectators as they dare to enter the icy water and revel in the New Year.

Newport Winter Festival This festival offers a break from the dreariness of winter for ten days in late January and early February. You can see fireworks, attend concerts and dogsled races, enter a snow-sculpting contest, and take a carriage ride through the wintry streets of the city.

Rhode Island Spring Flower and Garden Show Spring blooms early at the Rhode Island Convention Center in Newport. Each year a specific type of garden is featured.

Convergence—Annual Festival of the Arts This summer-long event is sponsored by the Providence Parks Department and features visual and performing arts, dance, music, and theater. A favorite among visitors is the sculptures displayed in Roger Williams Park and in downtown Providence. The festival features music to satisfy every taste—you can hear everything from chamber music to an Afro-Cuban band.

Polar Bear Plunge

Apponaug Village Festival Each June visitors can enjoy a flea market and craft show that brings out the best talent in Warwick. There are also pony rides and plenty of food.

Children's Day Kids get a chance to experience games of the past during this June celebration in Bristol. At the Coggeshall Farm Museum youngsters can play popular games of the eighteenth century, including ninepins, sticks and loops, and top spinning. It's a great day to enjoy some old-fashioned fun.

Summer Pops and Fireworks Music is in the air during the last part of June at the Wilcox Park grounds in Westerly. Past acts included the Chorus of Westerly and the Boston Festival Orchestra.

Newport Folk Festival Every August since 1958, Newport has hosted the very best in established and up-and-coming artists. Performers who have taken the stage include Bob Dylan, Joan Baez, James Taylor, Richard Thompson, and the Indigo Girls.

JVC Jazz Festival The second weekend in August brings the sound of jazz to Newport. For over 40 years, the best in traditional and modern jazz have shared their music and energy with Newport residents and visitors alike.

Harvest Fair In early October, a country fair in Middletown makes autumn a delight for visitors. Among the featured events are hayrides, sack races, a rope walk, and a greased pole climb—a challenge for everyone. Listen to local performers while sampling the baked goods and enjoying the crafts on display.

JVC Jazz Festival

Harvest by the Sea Festival During October, Newport County
residents enjoy apple cider and pumpkin-carving contests while
participating in the autumn whale watches. There's plenty to see
and do as the crisp air awakens everyone's appetite, which can be
satisfied at the farmers' market.

Montgolfier Day Balloon Regatta Hot-air balloons lend festivity and color
to the Providence sky in late November. The balloons are launched
from the statehouse lawn to the thrill of spectators. The regatta
commemorates the first manned balloon flight in Paris in 1783.

Christmas at Blithewold From Thanksgiving to Christmas, the Blithewold Mansion and Gardens in Bristol are aglow with the traditional finery of the holidays. You can see an 18-foot decorated evergreen tree, glowing wreaths, and an amazing spectacle of flowering plants and greenery.

Festival of Lights Celebrate an old-fashioned Christmas in Kingstown with hayrides, storytelling, and caroling, and tour the beautiful homes of North Kingstown during the month of December.

STATE STARS

William Alison (Bill) Anders (1933–   ) was a crew member of *Apollo 8*, which in 1968 became the first manned spacecraft to circle the moon. Anders was a longtime resident of Providence.

Leonard Bacon (1887–1954) was a poet who made his home in Peace Dale. He won the 1941 Pulitzer Prize in poetry for his collection *Sunderland Capture and Other Poems*.

Joseph Brown (1733–1785) was a renowned architect born in Providence. His First Baptist Meeting House, located in Providence, is considered among the finest examples of colonial architecture in American.

Moses Brown (1738–1836) launched the cotton manufacturing industry in America when, in Pawtucket, he built the first textile mill to use water power to manufacture cotton thread. He also led the effort to abolish slavery in Rhode Island. Brown was born in Providence.

Nicholas Brown (1729–1791) directed the family businesses, which included slave trading, distilling rum, and making iron products. Brown was instrumental in convincing state leaders to ratify the U.S. Constitution. He was influential in establishing Rhode Island College and provided much support to the college. It was named Brown University in honor of his son Nicholas Brown Jr.

Ambrose E. Burnside (1824–1881) served as a Union general during the Civil War. His inept command during the Battle of Fredericksburg led to a crushing Union defeat, but Rhode Islanders continued to like him. After the war they elected him governor three times. His name and facial-hair style are said to be the origin of the word *sideburns*.

Vincent A. "Buddy" Cianci Jr. (1941–), a popular six-term mayor of Providence, oversaw sweeping changes, beautification, and modernization in the city, amounting to a "Providence renaissance." Affable and energetic, he was also criminally corrupt, and was eventually sentenced to five years in prison.

George M. Cohan (1878–1942) is considered the father of musical comedy in the United States. A composer, producer, actor, songwriter, and playwright, he set musicals in America rather than in foreign lands. He won the Congressional Medal of Honor for his patriotic World War I song "Over There." Cohan was born in Providence.

Thomas Wilson Dorr (1805–1854) led an uprising that became known as Dorr's Rebellion. Dorr and his followers created a new state constitution, known as the People's Constitution, which gave voting rights to all white adult males.

Peter Farrelly (1956–) and **Bobby Farrelly** (1958–), brothers born in Cumberland, together have written and directed popular Hollywood comedies such as *Dumb and Dumber*, *There's Something About Mary*, and *Me, Myself and Irene*—all set partly in Rhode Island.

Jabez Gorham (1792–1869) was the father of Rhode Island's silverware industry. Born in Providence, he founded Gorham Manufacturing Company, which became the world's largest producer of sterling silver items.

Peter (right) and Bobby Farrelly

Nathanael Greene (1742–1786) rose through the ranks to become one of George Washington's ablest generals during the American Revolution. Declaring, "We fight, get beat, rise, and fight again," he commanded an army that harassed, bedeviled, and exhausted the larger English forces in North and South Carolina.

John Milton Hay (1838–1905) served as private secretary to President Abraham Lincoln. As U.S. secretary of state from 1898 to 1905, he helped formulate America's Open Door policy toward China. Hay graduated from Brown University, which later named a library in his honor.

Stephen Hopkins (1707–1785) represented Rhode Island in the Continental Congress and was among those who signed the Declaration of Independence; as he did so, his hand shook from

hand trembles, but my heart does

`or ten`
`the`
`odest`
`ovidence`

`was a`
`lived in`
`st known`
`Battle`
`lso`
`social`
`ed for`

Julia Ward Howe

Anne Hutchinson (c. 1600–1643) was a religious enthusiast and one of the founders of Rhode Island. Born in England, she immigrated to Boston in 1634. Her religious views caused problems for her, she was excommunicated from the Boston church and settled with her followers in Rhode Island.

Christopher Grant La Farge (1862–1938) was an architect who specialized in designing churches. Born in Newport, he ran the firm that designed the interior of Saint Paul the Apostle Church in New York City and the Cathedral of Saint John the Divine.

Jacob Lawrence (1907–) is a painter who often portrays historical events and social issues that have affected African Americans. His paintings show busy street scenes, pool halls, and men and women working. Although he was born in New Jersey, he spent a great deal of his life in Rhode Island. He is known as the patriarch of today's African-American painters.

Ida Lewis

Ida Lewis (1842–1911) was the lighthouse keeper on Lime Rock in Newport Harbor for thirty-nine years. Born in Newport, she was the daughter of a sea captain. During her career, she performed many rescues, beginning in 1858 when she saved four men whose boat had capsized. Susan B. Anthony reported Lewis's exploits in her suffrage newspaper the *Revolution*. Lewis was awarded a gold medal by Congress and a pension by the Carnegie Hero Trust Fund.

H. P. Lovecraft (1890–1937) was an important writer of horror and supernatural fiction. Born in Providence on College Hill near Brown University, he lived there most of his life, strolling the streets and savoring the city's colonial architecture. His stories—some of them based on dreams—were published in *Weird Tales* and other "pulp" magazines of the day. Many of them are set in a fictionalized New England that is prey to demonic cosmic forces.

David Macaulay (1946–   ) is a celebrated writer. Macaulay studied architecture at the Rhode Island School of Design, but his interests led him to write and illustrate books that inform his readers about the world around them. His books include *Cathedral*, *City*, and *Pyramid*. In 1988, he published *The Way Things Work*, a book that teaches how everyday things do what they're intended to do. In 1991, his book *Black and White* won the Caldecott Award for the year's best picture book. His entertaining, informative books appeal to both children and adults. Macaulay taught at the Rhode Island School of Design for ten years.

Horace Mann (1796–1859) is known as the father of American public education. He graduated as valedictorian from Brown University in 1819 and then began a distinguished career in education, leading the movement to make education accessible to every child. He also served as the first head of the Massachusetts state board of education.

Annie Smith Peck (1850–1935) was a feminist, mountaineer, and Greek scholar. Born in Providence, she became the first woman to attend the American School of Classical Studies in Athens. Later she taught Latin at Smith College. Peck began climbing the Alps at age 45 and was a founding member of the American Alpine Club in 1902. She climbed and traveled well into her eighties.

Oliver Hazard Perry (1785–1819) commanded ships in the Great Lakes during the War of 1812. His famous words, "We have met the enemy and they are ours," were issued after his heroic victory on Lake Erie in 1813. He was born in South Kingstown.

Samuel Slater (1768–1835) built America's first water-powered cotton-spinning machine in Pawtucket. Slater manufactured the machine based on his memory of machinery invented by Englishman Richard Arkwright. Thus began the American cotton industry.

Gilbert Stuart

Gilbert Stuart (1755–1828) painted portraits of noted people of his time, such as the first five presidents of the United States. He is best known for his portraits of George Washington, including the one that appears on the one-dollar bill, although he said he found the stiff, distracted Washington "most appalling to paint."

Chris Van Allsburg (1949–   ) is a writer and illustrator of children's books. Born in Michigan, he received a master's degree from the Rhode Island School of Design in 1975. He began teaching illustration there in 1977 and, although he is no longer teaching, he is still affiliated with the school. Van Allsburg has won Caldecott Medals for his illustrations for *Jumanji* and *The Polar Express*, both of which became popular films. In 1993, he won the Regina Medal in honor of his contribution to children's literature.

Roger Williams (c. 1603–1683) is regarded as the founder of Rhode Island. He advocated religious tolerance and democracy and wrote about his principles of religious freedom in *The Bloudy Tenent of Persecution* (1644). He maintained friendly relations with the Native Americans of the region after founding Providence in 1636. Williams served as president of Rhode Island colony after it was chartered in 1644.

Leonard Woodcock (1911–   ), an American labor leader and diplomat, was born in Providence. He became vice president of the United Automobile Works (UAW) in 1955 and was elected president of the UAW in 1970. In 1979 President Jimmy Carter named him U.S. ambassador to China.

TOUR THE STATE

Benefit Street (Providence) This mile of history includes an impressive array of colonial homes. Walking through this hilly district, you can see many eighteenth- and nineteenth-century houses.

Roger Williams Park Zoo (Providence) The more than one thousand animals at the zoo live in exhibits that re-create the African plains, the American tropics, and other regions. Children can enjoy special birthday parties at the zoo.

Roger Williams National Memorial (Providence) Built on the site of the original Providence settlement of 1636, this memorial features displays commemorating Williams's contributions to democracy and religious freedom, including an audiovisual presentation describing Williams's life.

Museum of Natural History Roger Williams Park (Providence) This museum contains an abundance of artifacts to delight visitors, including tools that whalers brought back from the South Pacific. The planetarium makes this museum doubly worth a stop.

The Arcade (Providence) This magnificent structure houses the nation's oldest shopping mall. Built in 1828, this marketplace still thrives and features international boutiques and eateries.

Statehouse (Providence) Modeled after the U.S. Capitol in Washington, D.C., this structure boasts the fourth-largest self-supporting marble dome in the world. A gold-covered statue of the Independent Man stands atop the dome to symbolize Rhode Island's history of religious freedom. Visitors can also view Gilbert Stuart's full-length portrait of George Washington.

Slater Mill Historic Site (Pawtucket) At this site, craft exhibits and working machinery tell the tale of the birth of the American industrial revolution. Among the exhibits is the nation's first water-driven cotton mill.

Roger Williams National Memorial

Green Animals Topiary Gardens (Portsmouth) Have you ever seen a shrub that reminded you of a giraffe? At this garden, you will see a giraffelike bush, along with 80 other sculptured trees and shrubs that look like camels, peacocks, wild boars, and other creatures. Next to these gardens is a museum featuring children's toys and furniture from the nineteenth century.

Norman Bird Sanctuary (Middletown) You can enjoy the breathtaking beauty of Rhode Island at this 300-acre area of ridges, valleys, and ponds, which include 7 miles of trails. The sanctuary is devoted to the protection of native plants and animals, and the preservation of unique landforms.

Newport Historical Society (Newport) Here visitors can view displays of documents and artifacts from the area's colonial days.

Hammersmith Farm (Newport) The only working farm in Newport, Hammersmith Farm was the childhood home of Jacqueline Kennedy Onassis and became known as the "summer White House" of President John F. Kennedy. Built in 1887, the 28-room cottage was the site of the Kennedys' wedding reception. It is not open to the public.

The Breakers (Newport) Visit the mansion where steamship and railroad tycoon Cornelius Vanderbilt lived. Built in 1895, this spectacular 70-room mansion was modeled after Italian villas.

Green Animals Topiary Garden

The Breakers

Adventureland (Narragansett) How would you like to visit an island, venture deep into a cave, and then drive a go-cart? You can do all this and more at this park, which also features an 18-hole miniature golf course and many lovely waterfalls.

Museum of Primitive Art and Culture (South Kingston) Here you can view art and artifacts made by American Indians as well as people from the South Seas and Africa.

Tomaquag Indian Memorial Museum (Exeter) This museum displays a large collection of local and regional Indian artifacts.

Gilbert Stuart Birthplace (Saunderstown) Located on a quiet back road, this charming eighteenth-century home and restored grist mill commemorates the colonial artist who painted the most famous portrait of George Washington. Stuart spent the first seven years of his life here.

Great Swamp Fight Monument (South Kingstown) This stone obelisk memorializes the Narragansett and Wampanoag Indians who were massacred during King Philip's War in 1675. The nearby Great Swamp Management Area has walking trails where visitors may see many varieties of wildlife, including mink, raccoons, deer, and owls.

South County Museum (South Kingstown) This museum contains more than 10,000 items from early Rhode Island life—everything from a country kitchen to a maritime display. Walk the nature trails and visit a historic cemetery before heading off to the many demonstrations and lectures that help visitors understand the life and times of rural Rhode Island long ago.

Quonset Air Museum (North Kingstown) If you like aircraft, a visit here is a real treat. Many military aircraft are on display, including a Russian MIG-17. You can also see aircraft in different phases of restoration as the staff works on upcoming exhibits.

Block Island A popular family vacation spot, this island features beautiful beaches, hiking trails, wildlife sanctuaries, and the lighthouses.

FUN FACTS

Rhode Island was the first free republic of the New World. The Rhode Island General Assembly formally declared the colony's independence from Great Britain on May 4, 1776. The other twelve colonies joined the cause two months later. The oldest synagogue in the United States is located in Newport. The Touro Synagogue was completed in 1763 and is still standing today.

Ann Franklin, Benjamin Franklin's sister-in-law, became America's first woman newspaper editor when she took over the *Newport Mercury* in 1762, after the death of its original editor, her son.

The Pawtucket Red Sox, a minor league team, played in the longest game in baseball history. It ran 32 innings on April 18, 1981, before being stopped. When it was resumed two months later, the PawSox won in the thirty-third inning, beating the Rochester Red Wings, 3-2.

Rhode Island is the only state that still celebrates V-J Day, marking the victory over Japan that ended World War II, because, according to one news report, the state's war veterans "obstinately refuse" to give up the tradition. Held on the second Monday in August, the state holiday is officially known as Victory Day.

Find Out More

If you would like to learn more about the Ocean State, look in your local library or bookstore or on the Internet. Here are a few titles to get you started:

GENERAL STATE BOOKS

Doak, Robin S. *Rhode Island* (Life in the Thirteen Colonies). Danbury, CT: Children's Press, 2004.

Warner, John F. *Rhode Island*. Minneapolis: Lerner Publications Company, 2003.

SPECIAL INTEREST BOOKS

Burgan, Michael. *Roger Williams: Founder of Rhode Island*. Mankato, MN: Compass Point Books, 2006.

Mcdermott, Jesse. *Voices from Colonial America: Rhode Island 1636–1776*. Washington, DC: National Geographic Children's Books, 2006.

WEB SITES

Narragansett Indian Tribe
www.narragansett-tribe.org
Information on the Narragansett Indians' history and present activities, some of it intended for members of the tribe.

The Providence Journal

www.projo.com

The *Providence Journal-Bulletin* Web site, with local news, commentary, and a live one-frame-per-minute camera view of various locations in downtown Providence.

Rhode Island

www.visitrhodeisland.com

All kinds of tourism information and trip-planning material are available here, courtesy of the Rhode Island Economic Development Corporation.

Index

Page numbers in **boldface** are illustrations and charts.

ABOUT THE AUTHOR

Ted Klein's family connections to Rhode Island date back to the 1870s, when the Kleins opened a rosary factory in Providence. Ted himself attended Brown University in Providence. Alhough he now lives in New York, working as a magazine editor and writing fiction, he keeps up with Rhode Island, his favorite state, through friends and family.